THE SMART WOMAN'S GUIDE TO BUILDING & PROTECTING WEALTH

The LAWS *of* YOUR MONEY

ANN-MARGARET CARROZZA, ESQ.

ALLWORTH PRESS
NEW YORK

Allworth Press books may be purchased in bulk at special discounts for sales promotion, corporate gifts, fund-raising, or educational purposes. Special editions can also be created to specifications. For details, contact the Special Sales Department, Allworth Press, 307 West 36th Street, 11th Floor, New York, NY 10018 or info@skyhorsepublishing.com.

30 29 28 27 26 5 4 3 2 1

Published by Allworth Press, an imprint of Skyhorse Publishing, Inc.
307 West 36th Street, 11th Floor, New York, NY 10018.

Allworth Press® is a registered trademark of Skyhorse Publishing, Inc.®, a Delaware corporation.

www.allworth.com

Cover design by Brian Peterson
Cover photo by Douglas Gorenstein

Library of Congress Cataloging-in-Publication Data is available on file.

Print ISBN: 978-1-62153-859-2
eBook ISBN: 978-1-62153-860-8

Printed in the United States of America

Table of Contents

Introduction

When money is a problem, *everything* is a problem. Getting our finances in order is always near the top of our New Year's resolutions. Unfortunately, most of us remain financial train wrecks. We are living in a litigious "gotcha" society. People can break into our homes and attempt to claim squatter's rights. Levels of consumer debt are out of control. The average person carrying debt works two months each year just to pay interest on their credit cards, mortgages, and student and auto loans. Is there any hope of regaining control? Not without some new approaches!

The premise of this book is that building, safeguarding, and sharing wealth are not only individually necessary activities, but they are also interdependent. Strategically and simultaneously tackling all three areas has the effect of turbocharging our wealth-building.

That being said, the reader may choose to begin this book with chapter 5 to focus immediately on asset-building activities. Here, I share lessons from my over twenty thousand clients on recognizing, marshalling, and deploying nontraditional assets to generate wealth. No matter how much or little we happen to have right now, we should all be working on growing wealth. Wealth is dynamic—like a shark that must constantly be moving. Lottery winners and other windfall recipients who stop actively growing their wealth may experience a "what now?" crisis that augurs a downward spiral, leaving many with less than they had before the big win.

It is only with proof that our assets are growing that we can banish "scarcity mentality." This, in turn, frees us up to joyfully share what we have with others. It is in this magical realm of sharing that yet more wealth will come our way.

Alternatively, one may begin with chapter 9 and immediately put the wealth-compounding effects of generous actions to work. Newton's Third Law of Motion tells us that for each action there is an equal and opposite reaction. This is not "woo-woo" stuff—this is physics. What we put out there (good or bad) will come back to us big-time!

I chose to start the book with wealth protection concepts. For me, there is logical appeal in ensuring that our piggy banks have no gaping holes before we set about filling them up! We need a well-planned structural base and solid legal infrastructure from which to build our fortunes. There can be no meaningful discussion of personal finance without legal protections!

After all, what does it matter how diligently I save and invest if there is a greater than 40 percent chance of losing assets to a long-term illness, divorce, lawsuits, and/or taxes? Yes, paying taxes is mandatory, but overpaying taxes is just plain stupid! Through dozens of cautionary tales, you will learn to identify and avoid the legal landmines lurking in your life.

The concept of something being greater than the sum of its parts is attributed to Aristotle, and a philosophical concept later known as emergence. An orchestra, for example, is exponentially more powerful than the individual contributions of the strings, woodwinds, percussion, and brass sections. As it relates to wealth, the three pillars of growth, protection, and sharing truly are interdependent. Putting regular simultaneous effort into all three cannot fail to produce powerful and lasting wealth.

1
There's a Lawsuit for That

Legal protections are the very foundation of personal finance. After all, what does it matter how well we save, invest, and grow our assets if we have a high statistical likelihood of losing much of it? We have a high statistical likelihood of losing assets to a long-term illness, expensive breakup, and myriad other legal liabilities. When it comes to criminal law matters, it is said that ignorance of the law is no excuse. When it comes to your money, ignorance of the law will get you steamrolled.

There have never been more theories of civil legal liability than we have today. It is hard to watch TV without seeing an ad for a law firm trolling for clients who have real or perceived grievances against someone. A sampling of recent lawsuits illustrates the litigious climate in which we live:

In Israel, a woman sued TV weatherman, Danny Rup, for a forecast that turned out to be wrong. Mr. Rup predicted a sunny day. The plaintiff claimed that she relied upon this information when selecting her attire for the day. She stated in her lawsuit that she was unprepared for the ensuing thunderstorms. Soaked to the skin, she caught the flu and missed four days of work. Desirous of avoiding a public trial, the station paid the plaintiff the equivalent of $1,000 and gave her an apology.

Closer to home, a deceased man's family sued SeaWorld for wrongful death following his attack by a killer whale. The backstory revealed that the decedent hid in the park past closing time and waited for staff to leave. He then indulged his lifelong fantasy of swimming with a whale. It seems that the whale was less enthused by the prospect, evidenced by the dead body discovered the following morning. The plaintiff acknowledged that the whale habitat clearly identified the denizens as "killer whales." The substance of the lawsuit was that SeaWorld failed to adequately warn against the possibility of the killer whales actually killing someone. While the suit was ultimately withdrawn, the defendant had to pay substantial legal fees.

Who among us has not had a horrible first date? A Texas man apparently felt that commiserating with friends over drinks about his rotten evening wasn't enough. He invoked the legal system to right his perceived injury. Brandon Vezmar's petition sought damages from his date because she was texting during the movie he paid for. He alleged that the unnamed woman "adversely affected the viewing experience . . ."

A few years back, I remember reading about a man in China filing suit against his wife on account of their child having been born "ugly." The suit alleged infidelity, because the man was certain that the parties could not have produced an "ugly" baby. After a DNA test confirmed that the plaintiff was, in fact, the father, it emerged that the defendant had several cosmetic surgical procedures before meeting the plaintiff. A sympathetic court ordered the soon-to-be-ex-wife to pay the equivalent of $120,000 in damages for "tricking the plaintiff into marrying her under false pretenses."

Remember the man who sued Anheuser Busch, because his consumption of Bud Light failed to conjure up a bevy of bikini-clad ladies? The plaintiff contended that the commercials depicting beautiful women on a beach surrounding a beer-guzzling man, amounted to false advertising. Although he was unsuccessful in court, lawsuits like these are no laughing matter to defendants forced to spend valuable time and resources on their defense.

Rosenberg v. Google involved a plaintiff's claim that walking directions from Google Maps resulted in her crossing a highway where she was struck and injured by a car.

Everyone has heard about the suit against McDonald's for a burn resulting from spilled coffee. Even though the damages were ultimately drastically reduced from the eye-popping amount awarded by the jury, it is important to remember that the defendant was forced to pay many thousands in legal defense costs.

Novel theories of civil legal liability abound. One example is "negligent infliction of emotional distress" as a stand-alone cause of action. Can someone now sue me because I was daydreaming and failed to say hello? Did this omission on my part cause him emotional distress? Was he with his new girlfriend and made to feel stupid when his cheerful greeting to me was not returned? Silly, you may say. I agree—but by the time I get a judge to see that it is silly, I may have spent thousands of dollars in legal fees.

I predict that we will soon see an uptick in workplace lawsuits. Consider the Kentucky man, who was awarded $450,000 after his coworkers threw him an office birthday party against his wishes. Maybe it was the prospect of a dry supermarket cake that prompted this man to beg his supervisor not to throw such a party. But when confronted with his undeterred coworkers serenading him in the break room, the plaintiff was nearly paralyzed with anxiety. He sought refuge inside his parked car. This was the beginning of the end of his employment. The court agreed that the employer was at fault here.

On a recent trip to California, I saw two separate law firm billboards trolling for clients who have been bullied at work or subject to a hostile workplace. What exactly is the employer's liability for Brenda in marketing eating Kelly from accounting's ramen noodles from the office kitchen—again?!

Trial lawyers are among the most effective lobbying groups at the state and federal level. The result is that there are legal theories of liability on the books that defy logic. Among these are the so-called scaffolding laws. In some jurisdictions, construction companies are on the hook for damages resulting from a worker's fall from scaffolding—no matter what. Did the plaintiff have a few beers at lunch before the fall? Doesn't matter—the company is on the hook!

Heightened liability costs for companies are ultimately passed on to consumers in the form of higher prices. The question of where to draw the line with theories of liability filled many hours of debate time during my service as a New York State legislator.

It is a fact that during times of economic uncertainty, more civil lawsuits are filed. As an asset-protection attorney, it is my job to educate clients on the potential areas of exposure and offer preemptive structural protections.

It is quite ironic that the granddaughter of a slip-and-fall master makes her living protecting people from such lawsuits. More than once, a family wedding with an open bar and a dance floor resulted in my grandmother falling. Perhaps the catering hall failed to properly warn guests that drunken dancing could result in a tumble? I do feel more than a little guilty that my braces were paid for, in part, by one of the ensuing legal settlements.

A major part of my law practice is to educate people about legally protecting their assets. Insurance alone does not cover all losses. When I suggest the use of a trust, limited liability company (LLC), partnership, or corporation to protect assets from liabilities, I invariably hear about the substantial property and casualty insurance policies in place.

As a general proposition, I am of the opinion that the insurance industry is among the most profitable of all businesses, for a few reasons. They are brilliant when it comes to influencing favorable legislation. This favorable legislation, in turn, allows them to write contracts that can be extremely one-sided. Heads they win, tails, we lose.

A very common example to illustrate the limits of insurance involves informal caregiving in the home. It is an exceedingly pervasive practice to have an informal or "off the books" arrangement with someone who comes into the home to clean or care for a child or older relative. Desirous of avoiding a bureaucratic to do, the parties agree that no taxes or other deductions will be withheld. In fact, many caregivers will insist that payments be made in cash, Venmo, PayPal, or by way of a check payable to cash.

What would happen if an informal caregiver under this arrangement cuts her hand while preparing a sandwich for your elderly father who lives in your home? Or trips down the basement stairs en route to do laundry? If there is an injury, there is a good chance that the caregiver can and will successfully sue you for substantial money damages.

What about the property insurance that you have been paying into for years? There is a clause within all such policies barring payment for claims arising from an illegal activity. In this case, the illegal (though commonplace) act is employing someone without paying into workers comp, disability, social security, etc. Isn't it better to think about these things and deal with them on the front end?

It is not my intention to be sanctimonious. For years, I engaged a gutter cleaner and stayed willfully ignorant about the legalities. I paid him in cash and seriously doubted that he carried liability insurance. We became friendly, and I enjoyed our discussions about our misbehaving dogs. One day, he called me out of the blue for legal advice. He tripped and fell off another client's roof and wanted to know if I would represent him in his lawsuit against the homeowner! It was a serious wake-up call for me. If this guy had taken a spill off my roof, my homeowner's policy would likely not have covered a dime.

Psychological reliance on our insurance coverage comes from focusing on the dollar limits of the policy. A million-dollar liability coverage policy may give a great sense of security. I encourage people, however, to familiarize themselves with their coverage exclusions. Not many people actually read their insurance policies. They are several hundred pages and designed to be painfully boring.

Does your insurance cover damages from dog bites? It may or may not. It may also have so-called dangerous breed exclusions. Common among these are pit bulls, rottweilers, German shepherds, and wolf-hybrid breeds.

The most important advice I can give anyone about property insurance coverage is that you must inform the company of changes to the title, use, and/or occupancy of the premises. I am all for saving money but failing to notify your insurer about an important change because you are afraid the premiums will go up can wind up costing you a bundle!

Following a parent's death, one of the notifications that must be made is to the home's insurer. If the house will be vacant during the months-long probate process (we discuss avoiding probate in chapter 2), you are required to notify the company. Failure to do so will result in denial of claims. Yes, the premiums to insure a vacant house will be high, but failure to notify the company effectively means that you have no coverage.

Another situation necessitating a call to your insurance agent is using a property as a rental. It is silly to try to save a few dollars by failing to disclose that tenants will be using a property. If you are considering short-term rentals, it is also critically important to familiarize yourself with the relevant zoning rules in your county or town. In recent years, many popular destinations have enacted 30-day minimum rental stays. This is in response to complaints by the year-round (voting) residents about havoc caused by short-term renters. If you flout the applicable rules, your insurer would be within its rights to deny a claim.

TAKEAWAY

We are living in a "gotcha" society. If we are serious about protecting what's in our wallets and bank accounts, we need to be aware of legal liabilities and implement protections. Keeping things simple and casual can end up being very expensive!

2

Keep Your Loved Ones Out of Probate Court

Effective legal planning can keep us out of court and will save our loved ones a lot of money! Bad or no estate planning costs families dearly. My own grandmother died without a will. This was not due to my lack of trying. I broached the subject, as a newly minted attorney, many years ago. It is the only time that I can recall her being really angry with me. She was decidedly "old school" and seemed to think that doing a will was akin to courting death. Turns out she was far from alone in this school of thought.

An estimated 49 percent of us have no will. The actor Chadwick Boseman was one of the many celebrities to have died without a will. When there is no will, the deceased's state of residence uses a formula to distribute their assets.

The problem is that these recipients of the assets may not be who the deceased would have chosen.

Simone Ledward, who Boseman married a few months before his untimely death, was entitled to everything by virtue of state law. Did the actor wish to leave anything to his surviving parents? We will never know. Fortunately for the parents, Ledward reportedly shared the estate with them. In my experience, this level of generosity is not common.

The musician Prince died in 2016 without a will. His estate was locked for years in battles between would-be beneficiaries and the IRS. Tens of millions were reportedly spent on legal fees, thereby resulting in far less for the ultimate heirs.

Everyone—even those without a will—knows what a will is. My will, at its essence, sets forth who gets my stuff upon my death. In theory, the concept could not be simpler. In practice, though, it's usually anything but simple.

Every state has laws dealing with what makes a will valid. If we run afoul of the statutory (written law) requirements, then a court can nullify all or part of the document. What does a court have to do with my will? Everything!

I tell my clients that we should all have a will. In terms of a "pecking order," it is better to have a will than not have a will. It is even better, though, to avoid having to rely upon the will to distribute my stuff at death. We want to have it as a fallback. Not as our primary distribution document. This is because a will is not "self-activating." The folks I name in the document cannot simply present it at my bank in order to receive the account proceeds that it says they are to inherit.

A will must first be authenticated by the court by way of an archaic process called probate before the named beneficiaries can receive their inheritance. The purpose of probate is to determine whether the will is valid. This necessitates a physical examination of the document. Does it appear to have been tampered with? Were the staples removed? The court must then satisfy itself that the person who created the document had requisite mental capacity and was free from duress.

How can the court know the state of mind of a person who is now dead? The sworn testimony of the witnesses to the will is needed, in order to establish that the formalities of the will execution were observed and that the person signing the will (the testator) was in his or her right state of mind.

The witnesses' testimony is needed to establish that the testator intended for the document in question to serve as his or her will. The probate process seeks to guard against evildoers tricking someone who has a cognitive impairment or had no idea what they were signing. A real-life example would be a rotten guy who told his elderly uncle that he could save some money with his internet and cable provider by signing the papers offered to him—and those papers had nothing to do with his internet and cable provider.

I am often asked why probate takes so darn long? The answer to this question is found in applicable state law. Each state has a minimum statutory period of time that the probate process must be open. In New York, this period is seven months. The idea is to give would-be creditors a chance to come forward and get paid out by the estate before it is distributed to the beneficiaries.

I was about to write that the process is rarely completed within seven months. I am generally allergic to speaking in absolutes. However, based on my twenty-plus years handling thousands of probate matters, I feel very safe in saying that probate is never completed that quickly.

One factor that drags out the process is the requirement that all of the testator's "heirs at law" be notified of the proceeding. Heirs at law are the folks who would inherit the estate in the absence of a valid will. These are sometimes called the "default takers." Your state legislators came up with a formula and a pecking order of beneficiaries who get your stuff if a valid will wasn't completed (or can't be found).

Generally speaking, a spouse and children share the estate. If the children are minors, the court will appoint a *Guardian ad Litem* (legal guardian) to oversee their interests (for a hefty fee paid from the estate).

Decedents with no spouse or children present more complexity. Courts have the discretion to require that a genealogist and even a detective be engaged to ensure that parents, brothers, sisters, and cousins are located and notified.

Wait a minute, you may say. These relatives are the ones who take in the absence of a will. Why, then, does the court have to notify and involve them if I *do* have a will?

The rationale for the requirement is that because they would take without a will, the law gives these people an opportunity to dispute the validity of the will. Heirs at law who are not mentioned in the will often have great incentive to interpose (introduce) objections to the propounded (put forth) will.

Am I not free to leave my stuff to whomever I wish? With the exception of a surviving spouse (unless they waived their right to inherit, in a valid prenup or postnup), this is true. However, all heirs at law must be notified. You haven't seen your cousins since Thanksgiving in 1978? The judge still wants them notified.

Sometimes the executor and named beneficiaries in the will think that they will get to the probate finish line quicker by telling the judge there is no way that these relatives can be tracked down, saying something like, "Heck, your honor, I don't even know if the folks are still alive."

This is a rookie mistake. The judge will then order that a genealogist and/or detective be hired to track these folks down. If they are, in fact, dead, then their surviving children and grandchildren become parties to the proceeding. Again, heaven help those hoping for speedy probate if any of these people are minors or incapacitated; a *Guardian ad Litem* will be appointed to safeguard their interests.

Whenever I see a will that lists beneficiaries other than a testator's heirs at law, I know we are in for a lengthy adventure. It is commonplace for the relatives who were not named in the will to lawyer up. They find attorneys, sometimes of questionable moral character, who take these cases on a contingency-fee basis. You see this in the context of ads for personal injury attorneys: "At the law firm of Rokm, Sokm, and Rekm, we don't get paid, unless you get paid."

Q: Should I leave an estranged relative $5 in the will to prevent a challenge to it?

A: No!

This is a pervasive but incorrect piece of homespun advice. Tiny bequests are very insulting to the person named. In my experience, such a bequest is more likely to precipitate a will challenge than leaving the person nothing.

A better alternative is to leave the potential objectant just enough that they would be afraid to lose. I might leave an estranged relative $10,000 in the will, which would also include a "no-contest" clause: "Anyone who institutes a challenge or objection to this will, forfeits their bequest hereunder."

Will Objections 101

The theories most commonly used to set aside a will are that the testator did not have the required mental capacity; that they signed by mistake (i.e., thought they were signing something else); or that they were subject to undue influence by the people named as beneficiaries in the will.

A natural (and logical) question is, "If these objecting relatives had not seen the testator in decades, how the #@*&! could they know about his mental state?" Of course, they can't possibly have any such information. In practice, objectants don't let a minor detail such as no facts get in the way of their case and hoped-for payday. Through attorneys, they simply recite every possible reason for objecting to the will. The burden then shifts to the attorneys for the named executor to demonstrate that the testator had capacity, and that the "execution ceremony" (little changed for centuries) was legit.

Witnesses to the will need to be located to offer testimony about the testator's mental state. They will be asked what the testator was wearing that day, did she have reading glasses on when she signed, etc. If the witnesses respond with too many "ums" and "I'm not sures" the will could be in trouble.

Do I Need an Attorney to Write My Will?

My husband needs a knee replacement. He is putting off seeing a surgeon. His justification goes something like this: "If I ask a surgeon if I need surgery, hmmm, I wonder what the answer will be?"

Yes, this attorney does believe that an attorney should be involved in the preparation of the will. I don't say this in order to protect the turf of my profession. In fact, I strongly and loudly encourage people to do their own health care proxies and a few other documents. (Free documents are on my website for your use: mylawyerann.com.)

The will, however, is a very different matter. The laws of most states say that "a will executed under the supervision of an attorney is presumed to be valid." Yes, probate is still a lengthy and often painful process, but the upshot of this statute is best understood by looking at what it does not say. In other words, if a will done by an attorney is presumed to be legitimate, what does that imply about a will not done by an attorney? A lot—and that a will that is created without an attorney is illegitimate is just one possibility.

Yes—as a technical matter, anyone is free to do their own will. I understand the logical appeal to someone who tells me that they can copy their friend's will and simply copy-and-paste their loved ones' names into the existing document. What is the difference between the two identical documents, other than the fact that one just happened to have been done by a lawyer? This is a very good question.

Yes, you are legally able to write your own will. In fact, you are free to write it on a pizza box. In law school we learned about a case where a will written inside of a kitchen cabinet was upheld by the court. This is a technically correct answer: you can write your own will.

The problem in real life is that a "homemade will," no matter how perfect it may look, will be tied up in the probate process much longer than a will done by an attorney. Without the statutory presumption of legitimacy afforded to attorney-prepared wills, the court can and will subject the homemade will to a heightened level of scrutiny (and subsequent delays!).

Aretha Franklin's estate was tied up in court for years. Her surviving loved ones were pitted against each other fighting over which of her handwritten wills (one was discovered under a couch cushion) with numerous cross-outs should be considered valid.

Probate Is a Public Process

Regardless of who creates the will, its administration through the probate process is open to the public. Any member of the public is free to go to probate court (called surrogate's court in many areas) and ask to see any will. That is how we all know so much about the legal and financial affairs of deceased celebrities.

There are many reasons to want to avoid probate. This is especially true if there is any level of complexity within your family. If, for example, there is an estranged relative who could cause a problem, or if we are leaving our beneficiaries unequal amounts. Louis and Marie's family learned this the hard way.

MEET LOUIS AND MARIE

Louis and Marie had two daughters, Leanna and Tina. The daughters each struggled with mental health issues. Tina never left home, was unemployed, and received a monthly SSI (Supplemental Security Income) check. She gave some of her modest monthly income to her parents as rent. Leanna had previously owned her own home but moved back in with Louis and Marie, with her two children, after a second divorce and subsequent home foreclosure.

When Louis and Marie were ready to do their wills, they decided that their situation was not complicated enough to involve a lawyer, who might charge a few hundred dollars. In their minds, they were too smart to waste money on legal fees, as so many of their friends had done. Louis's sister generously sent him the unsigned draft version of her own will done by her attorney. Louis saved the document and replaced the names with his family members.

In terms of the distribution in the wills, they naturally opted to leave everything to the surviving spouse upon the first death. Upon the second death, however, they decided against an equal division between Leanna and Tina. A rough mental calculation of all the money Louis and Marie had given to Leanna over the years easily exceeded the value of their current estate. They had paid for the weddings, the divorces, the down payment on Leanna's house, as well as for private school tuition for her kids, Hailey and Mason. Surely Leanna would understand that this was fair. They agreed not to talk to their daughters about the wills so as not to upset them with morbid thoughts.

Where do you think these geniuses stored the will? In Marie's lingerie drawer! So, one day while Louis and Marie were at their weekly church bingo game, Leanna was rifling through drawers for money and found and read the will. The entire estate would, one day, be left to Tina! She wanted to kill someone. In fact, she wanted to kill several people.

Leanna resisted the impulse to angrily confront her parents. She was sure that Tina had put them up to this. They must have felt sorry for poor pathetic Tina. She decided to say and do nothing until she could figure out a plan.

Some days later, it came to her. She would simply destroy the will. Tina never ventured outside of the house, so Leanna took the will and burned it in the woods.

Years later, when Louis and Marie had died, no one could find a will. The estate, therefore, was distributed equally to Leanna and Tina, based on their state's default distribution formula. Would they have been better off going to a lawyer, who would have urged them against storing the potentially explosive document in the home? You know my answer to this question.

The Louis and Marie saga is but one of many thousands of examples of estate plans that are a "penny wise and a pound foolish." Yes, the couple did save a few hundred bucks with their homemade will. The cost to Leanna and Tina, however, was many thousands of dollars, by way of the court-supervised intestate estate administration.

Once the estate assets were finally in the hands of Leanna and Tina, what do you think happened to Tina's SSI benefits? The inheritance disqualified her from eligibility for the program. If Marie and Louis had sat down with a good attorney, they would have been advised on creating a supplemental needs trust. This trust could have enabled Tina to benefit from the estate while remaining eligible for her program benefits. Marie and Louis's DIY estate plan ended up costing the family a small fortune.

Avoid This Trap for the Unwary

When it comes to paying bills on a decedent's home during the probate process, it stands to reason that several expenses can be eliminated. Cable TV, internet, newspaper, and other monthly subscriptions come to mind as payments to stop. We do, however, need to keep paying property taxes, utilities (so pipes don't freeze), and as discussed earlier, homeowner's insurance.

Contrary to popular belief, there is no minimum asset threshold below which a family can avoid a court proceeding to transfer a decedent's assets. Let's say I own a home worth $400,000 at my death, but there is a mortgage on it for $380,000. Will my family have to probate my will to claim the $20,000 in equity? Without a trust in place, the answer is yes.

What if I also have credit card and student loan combined debt of $40,000? Now, the net value of my estate is negative. Will my family still have to go through probate to access the $20,000 of equity in my home? Technically, yes. However, in this example, the credit card and student loan debt must be satisfied, thereby rendering the estate administration exercise unappealing. Folks in this situation may simply wish to pack their toothbrushes and move on. The question is, can they? Are family members legally responsible for the debts of a deceased relative?

As a general rule, survivors are not legally responsible for the debts of a deceased loved one. The creditor is generally limited to presenting their claim to the estate of the decedent, as opposed to the ultimate beneficiaries. The law seeks to give creditors every chance possible to collect on their debts. As pointed out earlier, the estate must remain open for at least seven months to give creditors a chance to come forward.

In addition, the named executor (person in charge of probating the will) or administrator (person in charge of an administration proceeding if there is no will) is required by law to notify the court of any creditors that they have reason to know about. Payment of debts generally comes off the top of the estate as do expenses of administration such as the (substantial) attorney and court fees. The ultimate beneficiaries, whether named in the will or by state law, then split what's left over. Note that a well-thought-out estate plan may alter how debts are apportioned. More on that later.

Failure to properly deal with possible creditors can expose the named executor to personal liability. Let's say an executor distributes the estate equally to the four named beneficiaries in the will after given the green light by the court. Three months later, a doctor's bill comes in the mail. The executor here better hope that the other beneficiaries are nice people and will each chip in an equal amount to pay the bill. If they refuse, then the named executor or administrator could be personally liable for the debt.

What About Debts When There Is No Court-Supervised Estate Proceeding?

Let's say that my mother had no real estate. She rented her home. Upon her death, her only assets were bank accounts that listed me and my sister as the beneficiaries. What happens if, after we have divided and received the money, I get a phone call about a large debt my mother owed? Are my sister and I legally responsible to pay the bill?

That depends. In general, the answer is no. A decedent's creditors are usually limited to pressing their claims against an actual estate (court-supervised probate or administration). If the only assets were those that "passed by operation of law" (were automatically distributed because of a listed beneficiary or surviving joint owner, or through a trust), then as a technical matter there is no estate from which creditors must be paid. Naturally, moral obligations may warrant some attempt to pay or settle the debt. Here, I am simply telling you what the actual law is.

There are some exceptions to a creditor being limited to suing only an actual estate. The most notable exception is if a surviving loved one served as a guarantor or co-signed for the debt or loan. Common examples of this are when a survivor co-signed for a decedent's student loan or home mortgage. Death of the primary borrower pushes the co-signer into first place in terms of being liable for the debt.

There is another way that creditors can try to sue direct beneficiaries without having to pursue the estate. They try to get the beneficiary to acknowledge the debt. In other words, they attempt to get a person who is not liable for the debt to voluntarily undertake that liability. Sounds mean and weird, right? Unfortunately, it happens all the time.

One of the many pieces of advice that I give clients after the death of a loved one is "Don't answer your phone." Let every call go to voicemail and call back only those people you wish to speak with. This is because creditors will find you, they will call you, and they will try to trick you. Remember, we are talking about grief-stricken relatives, who may not be thinking clearly. The conversation goes something like this:

> "Hello." "Is this Maura Mahon?"
>
> "Yes."
>
> "My name is Amanda Gibbons. I am so terribly sorry about the loss of your mother."
>
> "Thank you so much."
>
> "I understand that your mother chose you to wrap up her final affairs and see to all details—is this right?"
>
> Now at this point, Maura may be wondering how Ms. Gibbons knew her mother. She isn't rushing her off the phone, because as far as she knows at this point, they may have played bridge together or belonged to the same church choir.
>
> "Maura, I do hope it is ok if I call you by your first name?"
>
> "Of course."

"Thanks so much. I am sorry to bring this small issue up, but I am sure that we can work something out. You see, your mother owes my client, Sarah's Safaris, $5,000 for her recent trip."

"My mother became ill and never went on the trip. We were hoping the money she already paid could be refunded."

"Oh dear. Unfortunately, your mother did not choose to purchase our recommended vacation insurance which would have waived her final payment and entitled her survivors to receive a refund of all payments made. The contract your mother signed makes it very clear that my client is entitled to full payment. Now Maura, I am sure that you would not want your dear mother's memory tarnished by a failure to honor her legal obligations. And I am truly sorry to have to be the one to bring this to your attention. I know that you are a responsible person. When I was looking for your contact information online, I saw wonderful pictures of you at Girl Scouts and Little League. You have such a wonderful looking family."

"Ms. Gibbons, I am a bit overwhelmed at the moment. Can I look into this and get back to you?"

"Maura, I completely understand. The thing is that there will be late fees and penalties added to the amount owed if we can't come to a resolution now. I'll tell you what—how about I arrange that you only have to pay $25 per month and we can resolve the whole matter?"

"Well, I guess that would be okay."

With those last words, Maura walked right into the trap laid out by the debt collector. The law provides that those not otherwise responsible for someone else's debt become responsible once they agree to pay it. Debt collectors know this and try to manipulate grieving loved ones into agreeing to reasonable sounding monthly payments. By agreeing to pay $25 per month, Maura instantly became liable for the entire amount due.

As I write this, my husband is being called several times a week by his late aunt's landlord for her back rent. Aunt Effie died with absolutely no assets to speak of. Somehow, the landlord tracked my husband down, and I know they are trying to trick him into acknowledging the debt.

TAKEAWAYS

- If you own real estate, you need something more than a simple will to stay out of probate court.
- Screen your phone calls in the aftermath of a loved one's death, and never agree to pay their debts with your money.

3

Zen and the Art of Trusts

"Put not your trust in money, but put your money in trust," counseled Oliver Wendell Holmes over one hundred years ago. The advice remains sound, provided you educate yourself enough about trusts and select the right one for your situation. Properly implemented, a trust will save your estate, and consequently your family, a lot of money.

Everyone has heard the term trust. For most people I speak with, the concept is murky and generally misunderstood. I believe that a trust has a place in *everyone's* financial life. I also believe that everyone is capable of understanding trusts at a level above the average attorney out there.

Let's start with what a trust is not. I hear people use "trust fund" interchangeably with the concept of a trust as a legal document. A "trust fund" is in our collective consciousness as the province of super wealthy people with yachts and castles. Our exposure to the term came from old movies and TV shows. I recall Thurston Howell III mentioning his trust fund on *Gilligan's Island.* We are not now focusing on trust funds.

Trusts are not just for wealthy families. More than 60 percent of Americans own a home. Without a trust, following their deaths, their families will have to go through the court-supervised probate or administration proceeding discussed earlier.

It is my hope that you are in agreement that the probate process should be avoided. It costs the estate a great deal of money, while simultaneously setting the stage for friction between surviving loved ones. Avoiding probate is easily accomplished with many types of assets. Life insurance, annuities, bank accounts, brokerage accounts, and retirement accounts are all assets that allow the holder to name a beneficiary. Upon the holder's death, the named beneficiary simply contacts the financial institution, presents a death certificate, and is very quickly in possession of the funds. This is because beneficiary designations usually trump the provisions in a will.

Let's say, for example, that I leave my Chase savings account to my niece, Cecilia, in my will. However, when I opened the account, I wrote the name of my other niece, Colette, on the beneficiary form. Who do you think is legally entitled to the Chase account proceeds? In this case, Colette will be the victor, and my estate saved money in court and legal fees because probate was avoided. However, my failure to regularly review all aspects of my financial and estate planning will result in turmoil for my surviving loved ones.

The one asset class that routinely pushes families into a court-supervised estate administration process is real estate. If

I don't make special arrangements, then my primary residence, vacation property, and any investment real estate can only pass to my beneficiaries upon the conclusion of the months-long probate or administration process.

Let's say that I leave my house to my daughter in my will. Shortly after my death, a neighbor offers her an all-cash deal at a great price for his son who is relocating to the area. If the neighbor is not willing to wait for the probate to be completed, then my daughter will unfortunately have to pass on this offer. Not only is she unable to sell the home, but she must also find the money to pay all expenses, such as property taxes, homeowner's insurance, utilities, etc. Many months of paying these expenses can really add up.

By contrast, with a good trust in place, my daughter is the legal owner of the property at the moment of my death. She is then free to sell it immediately.

What Is a Trust?

Unlike a will, a trust is not a testamentary document, which takes effect only at death, and only after the court is satisfied that it's legit. A freestanding trust, by contrast, is a legal agreement, like a contract, which is one hundred percent effective during a person's life. Therefore, there is no need for court oversight or administration upon the person's death. A (properly drafted) trust, unlike a will, is immediately effective upon death.

OK, you say, but what IS it?

At its essence, a trust is a legal agreement between the person creating the document, called the creator, trustor, settlor, or grantor; the person or people who serve as the manager or administrator, called the trustee(s); and the people who will ultimately benefit from the structure, called the beneficiaries.

Once created and funded, the assets now owned by the trust will be managed, invested, and distributed in accordance with whatever terms are contained in the document. Just like board games have their own specific rules, so too do trusts. The best way to really understand the concept of a trust is to explore a couple of the various trust structures out there.

REVOCABLE TRUSTS

A revocable or living trust is, hands down, the most widely known and used type of trust. Chances are pretty good that you have been invited to a seminar promoting these trusts. My mother is a regular attendee for the free refreshments. The concept is straightforward.

With a living or revocable trust, I can be my own trustee. I can transfer assets into the trust, and I can also remove assets from the trust whenever I wish. This is psychologically appealing to my inner control freak. Not many of us are eager to surrender control over our stuff during life. Upon my death, all assets in the revocable trust will go to my named beneficiaries without the dreaded probate process.

MEET LISA AND JANE-MARIE

Lisa and Jane-Marie were their parents' sole beneficiaries and coexecutors of the will. Somewhere during the eight months of probate, they decided to rent out their parents' house in order to generate some money to pay necessary carrying costs, such as property taxes. Their lawyer told them that they were not yet technically the owners of the house and were not exactly free to enter into a lease with a tenant. But they found some college students who were willing to rent the home for cash and didn't require a written lease. Jane-Marie and Lisa offered a discounted monthly rent.

Fortunately for the sisters, no one was injured on the property and the college kids paid their rent and amicably vacated the property once the probate proceeding was finally over. At this point, their lawyer asked if they would be selling the house. They were not quite ready to part with what was their childhood home. Moreover, their recent positive experience as landlords encouraged them to consider renting out the property to supplement their respective retirement incomes. The lawyer correctly pointed out that they should change the deed. If they were listing the property for sale, then they would simply create a deed in favor of the purchasers in their capacity as the estate's executors. However, with the probate done and no sale in the offing, a deed reflecting the current ownership was in order.

Prior to creating the new deed, the lawyer asked the sisters whose name should appear first on the deed. They agreed to list Jane-Marie first because she was older. The new deed was created and filed. The sisters soon had a new tenant in the house paying fair market value rent. Everything was great. Until it wasn't.

One morning, the tenant's overnight guest tripped down the front steps as she left the house. What should have been a two-minute "walk of shame" to her car was instead an ambulance ride to the hospital with a broken leg. It should go without saying that multiple lawsuits were promptly filed.

Remember: When you change the deed, it is critically important to notify the insurer.

Lisa and Jane-Marie hadn't notified the insurer, but they had other legal problems. Even if they had notified the insurance company when the lawyer changed the deed from their deceased mother's name into their joint names, the sisters and their families still had legal exposure.

They each had wills providing that their respective children inherit all assets upon death. Lisa tragically died only two years after her mother. Her children contacted a lawyer to begin the process of probating Lisa's will. All of Lisa's bank accounts listed the children as beneficiaries. The accounts, therefore, passed by operation of law, or automatically. They reasoned that they would then only need the probate process to transfer Lisa's one-half of the rental property.

When the probate attorney looked at the deed listing Lisa and Jane-Marie as owners, he had some unsettling news. Lisa's half-ownership went to Jane-Marie by virtue of the wording in the deed. Like the bank accounts, Lisa's interest in the real estate passed automatically. Unfortunately for the kids, though, it did not pass to them. Why and how did this happen?

Remember when the original lawyer asked the sisters how they wished the new deed to read?

Which name being listed first was the least important question to be asked. The way he wrote the deed was as follows: "Jane Marie and Lisa as Joint Tenants with Rights of Survivorship."

Legally, upon the death of Lisa, her interest passed automatically or "by operation of law" to her sister, Jane-Marie. Just like the beneficiary designation on a bank account, jointly owned real estate with a "survivorship" provision will always trump the provisions of the will. Lisa's children will now be totally dependent upon their aunt's sense of fairness. Jane-Marie has no legal duty to give Lisa's children half of the property. Moreover, even if she does the right thing, there will be gift tax consequences. This is because there is an annual cap on what you can gift another person, free of gift tax considerations. As of this writing, the annual gift tax exclusion is $19,000 per person.

A better, though still imperfect, form of real estate ownership for the sisters would have been: Jane-Marie and Lisa as "tenants in common." These three silly words make all the difference between Lisa's kids inheriting her half of the house or not. The tenants-in-common form of ownership means that the two halves of the real estate are legally separate. Upon the death of one owner, his or her interest does not pass automatically to the surviving owner. Instead, the decedent's interest passes to his or her "estate," where it will go through probate (if the person has a will) or administration (if the person had no will). This would have been a better result for Lisa's kids because they would not have been accidentally disinherited. It is far from ideal, though, because there is a lengthy court proceeding needed to transfer the property into their names.

If Lisa's half of the house had been owned by a living revocable trust, then her kids would have received her interest in the property immediately and automatically upon her death, with no delays or court process involved.

Let's go back in time and change the facts so that Lisa orders a living revocable trust kit online. She has her nephew, who is a law student, create a new deed showing Jane-Marie owns one-half and Lisa's revocable trust owns the other half. How lucky to have a law student in the family—he wouldn't even accept the $50 offered to him for his time!

Lisa then followed the trust instruction pamphlet and listed her children's names in the blank space provided. She then puts everything in the dining room buffet where she keeps her important papers. You can tell that we are headed toward a problem.

In this scenario, Lisa's kids still have to go through a court-supervised probate or administration proceeding. It was not enough to create the trust and create the new deed. The crucial missed step here was actually recording the deed with the applicable county clerk. Some deeds can be recorded after death. Not in this situation, though, because no one could find the deed!

Immediately after I took the bar exam, people pointed out that I would never know more about so many areas of law than I did at that moment. This was true. What was also true is that I knew next to nothing about the actual practice of law. In my first job as an associate attorney, I became good friends with one of the legal secretaries. She was very bright. I asked her if she ever thought about going to law school.

"Why would I?" she mused. "I make more than you associates."

Yep, I learned (at happy hour) that she was making more than twice my early-career salary. Several months in, I agreed that the disparity was warranted. So, it would not surprise me in the slightest if Lisa's nephew had been a constitutional law scholar. The practical upshot, though, is that he probably didn't know how or why the executed deed also needed to be recorded.

Simply having a revocable trust is not enough. You must actually ensure that ownership of your assets have been legally transferred into the trust. Otherwise, the document is nothing more than a worthless collection of printed pages.

To recap, a living revocable trust that has been properly funded and documented will avoid probate. This will save your loved ones a great deal of their time as well as a great deal of their money.

Does it not then stand to reason that everyone should have a revocable trust? That depends upon one's individual situation.

To the extent that a revocable trust allows me to avoid probate without requiring me to surrender control, it seems like a no-brainer. Indeed, promoters nationwide make a small fortune selling living revocable trusts. You can also save some money by buying lower cost DIY trust kits online or through your favorite home shopping channel.

If avoiding probate is the only goal, then a revocable trust is the way to go. If, however, I also want to confer some degree of legal protection on my stuff in the trust, I should consider another legal structure.

Think about it for a minute. To the extent that I am my own trustee of the revocable trust, I can access everything in it whenever I wish. Well, if I can get my hot little hands on the stuff whenever I want, does it follow that anything in the trust is protected *vis a vis* my creditors?

Of course not! If I can freely get the stuff, then so can creditors!

Avoiding probate, as I hope you will now agree, is a very good idea! However, not all methods of avoiding probate are created equal. Consider Rich and Fred's story.

Rich was a widower living in Oceanside, New York, with his adult daughter, Kelly. He and his neighbor, Fred, attended a seminar at the local VFW touting the wonders of living revocable trusts. Following the seminar, Rich scheduled an appointment to meet with the presenting attorney. Fred was not in a rush to make an appointment. When Rich told him about the legal fees involved to set the trust up, Fred felt that he dodged a bullet.

Rich went ahead with the trust to protect his daughter in the future. Fred also wanted to protect his family but was convinced that he could protect his assets and avoid probate in a simpler and cheaper manner. He found a local real estate attorney who transferred the deed to the house into the names of his three adult children. Fred was proud that he saved a few thousand dollars.

Five years later, Rich had a stroke. He had Medicare and an excellent Medicare supplement policy which covered nearly all hospital costs.

Following the hospitalization, Rich was not able to come home and, instead, went into a nursing home. Much to his daughter Kelly's dismay, Medicare and the supplement policy only covered the first 100 days of care. Following this, there were monthly bills in excess of $10,000! Rich's savings was depleted in a matter of months.

Kelly asked the social worker at the nursing home to help apply for Medicaid coverage as there was no money left. After gathering and sorting through all of the necessary financial records, the social worker advised Kelly to sell the house to pay for Rich's care. Kelly told her that she was mistaken. The house was protected by a trust. She hurriedly drove to the attorney's office where the trust was set up. Kelly asked the attorney to confirm that the social worker was wrong and that the house was protected from her father's exorbitant long-term care costs. It was then that Kelly learned the sobering truth that the house was protected only in the sense that it would be exempt from probate after her father's death. It was not protected from health care or any other claims during Rich's life. To the extent that Rich retained one hundred percent access to the assets in the revocable trust, they were one hundred percent available to his creditors. (Note that most states confer varying degrees of nursing home protection on one's primary residence. However, the home loses any such protection when the owner is permanently in a nursing facility.)

Kelly had to sell the house. Only when the sale proceeds had been totally consumed by the nursing home bills did Medicaid pick up the costs of care. In this case, Rich and Kelly ended up with the very same result as they would have without a revocable trust. The house would have to be sold either way to pay for the nursing home. The singular benefit of the trust, which is avoiding probate, becomes a moot point if the house must be sold before death to pay a nursing home.

Remember that a revocable trust will avoid probate on the assets it owns. It will not, however, confer any liability protection on the assets it contains.

Did Fred's low budget plan produce better results for his family? Let's see. Recall that Fred wanted to keep things simple and cheap. He transferred the home to his children. He was sure that they would view their names on the deed as a mere technicality and would continue to regard the home as belonging to Fred.

Shortly after the new deed was recorded, a letter came to the house from the county tax assessor's office. Apparently, the property was no longer entitled to Fred's homeowner's tax exemption or his partial veteran's exemption. He was no longer the owner of record, so his property taxes went up significantly.

Next, Fred's college-age grandchildren qualified for less college financial aid because one-third of the home's value had to be listed on the financial aid applications as belonging to their parents (Fred's children).

Then, Fred's daughter got divorced. Her one-third interest in the home was tacked onto her asset list, during the property-distribution phase of the divorce proceeding. Again, even though a gifted or inherited asset is technically off limits in a divorce, the judge in an "equitable distribution" state can look at the asset and then give the other party more of something else that can be distributed.

Fred briefly considered selling the home and moving to a warmer climate. The idea was quickly scuttled when the accountant pointed out that Fred would no longer benefit from his $250,000 capital gains tax exclusion upon sale.

"Let me guess," said Fred. "It's because the house is no longer in my name . . . ?"

Though not what I would call a quick study, Fred did come to realize that there were some real downsides to giving the house to the kids. He comforted himself with the notion that, at least, the home would be off-limits if he needed nursing home care. As it turned out, Fred died in his sleep one night without ever having needed a nursing home.

Because the house was already in the children's names, they did not have to go through a court supervised probate or administration proceeding. This was a relief to the children. They listed the house for sale right away and accepted an offer of $550,000. They were thrilled.

That is, until they did their taxes the following spring. It was only then that they learned the tax consequences of a completed gift made during one's life: When we make a completed gift of an appreciated asset (something that is now worth more than what we paid for it) during life, the new owner (recipient of the gift) takes the asset with a so-called cost basis equal to that of the donor's (the gift giver) original purchase price.

In this case, Fred bought the home in 1978 for $50,000 after his divorce from the kids' mom. That means that the three children had to pay capital gains taxes on approximately $500,000, which was the difference between the original purchase price and the ultimate sale price. The saddest part for the kids was when their accountants told them that Fred could have easily prevented this massive tax hit if he had done some better planning.

A simple gift of the house to the kids was very clearly not the way to go. Fred's declared objective was to keep things simple and low budget. In reality, he suffered from intellectual laziness. He couldn't be bothered to learn about the various asset protection options available to him. As for the money saved with his bargain estate plan, his kids ended up paying through the nose for this costly error. Yes, it requires a bit of active input to learn and process estate planning and asset protection concepts. And yes, there are fees charged by advisors. At the end of the day, though, we can protect assets from health care and other liabilities while also saving our loved ones a bundle in taxes.

Moreover, learning new things helps keep our brains youthful and elastic. Am I suggesting that visiting me for estate planning will stave off cognitive decline? I will not go quite that far (in writing). Suffice it to say that once you have embarked on the process and see what's possible, you will feel very good about the gift in terms of saved time, money, and stress for your loved ones.

Alternatives to a Revocable Living Trust

I hope that we are all on the same page with respect to the advisability of avoiding probate. We established that a properly funded revocable trust will, indeed, avoid probate. However, as the foregoing examples illustrate, there are a number of worthy goals in addition to avoiding probate. At a minimum, we want the legal structures we establish to protect assets from our own health care and other liabilities. We should also strive to protect assets from our loved one's future possible liabilities.

Examples of legal structures used for asset protection include corporations, partnerships, limited liability partnerships (LLPs), and limited liability companies (LLCs). These structures all have a place in the planning world, and I use them regularly. They are not however, my primary "go-to" structure. LLCs, LLPs, and corporations are not in and of themselves immune to long-term care costs, nor will they avoid the need for probate. My go-to primary structure is always a trust.

Didn't I just say that a trust was flawed? No, I said that a revocable trust alone will accomplish no more than avoiding probate. What I am suggesting is that you acquaint yourself with stronger trust varieties that can protect assets. Here are some examples.

LIFE INSURANCE TRUST

Life insurance nearly always avoids probate, thanks to the beneficiary designation on the policy. We only have issues in this regard when the named beneficiary has died, is ill, is a minor, or has psychiatric or developmental issues complicating their relationship with money.

It is important to regularly review your beneficiary designation to ensure that those named are in reasonably good health and able to manage money. If they aren't, you may wish to consider additional planning for them, which we will cover further on.

So, if the life insurance death benefit nearly always avoids probate, why do we need a life insurance trust? There are two reasons. First, we want to protect the value of the policy (here we are referring to the cash value of a whole life or universal policy) from health care costs and other liabilities during life. We also want to prevent our named beneficiaries from having to pay estate taxes on the benefits they receive upon my death.

Wait a minute, you say—the insurance salesman very clearly said that there are no taxes on life insurance. This is sort of true. There are no income taxes payable on life insurance proceeds. The value grows income-tax free and is not reportable on the ultimate beneficiary's income tax return.

The life insurance death benefit is not, however, free from estate taxes. This is somewhat ironic because a lot of people buy the policies in order to give their estate beneficiaries liquidity with which to pay any estate taxes imposed at death. This payment source, though, adds to the total tax due when the policy is owned by the decedent.

At its essence, a life insurance policy has three components: The owner, the "measured life," and the ultimate beneficiary. In order to protect the value of the policy from liabilities during life and from estate taxes at death, it is advisable to transfer the ownership of the policy into a properly drafted life insurance trust. The purchaser of the policy will remain the "measured life" and the beneficiaries can be anyone at all. They will now, though, technically be beneficiaries of the life insurance trust as opposed to being named on the actual policy. Please note that this is a very topical treatment of life insurance trusts. I am simply aiming to familiarize you with the usefulness of the structure.

As a general rule, the IRS becomes sad, for lack of a better term, when they miss out on estate taxes, that they would be getting in the absence of a trust. They channel this sadness into trying to pull the trusts apart during an audit. If the trust is not properly—and I would even say perfectly—drafted, then it can be set aside. A common reason that life insurance trusts are set aside is that the person creating the trust has retained too much power or control. A life insurance trust should *never be revocable.*

A life insurance trust should never be revocable, nor should it be a DIY project. Don't you think it's worth it to spend some money on legal fees to prevent your $2.0 million life insurance death benefit from being subject to 40 percent in estate taxes? I know I do.

TRUST FOR REAL ESTATE

If we seek to avoid probate and confer some measure of asset protection upon our real estate, then we need a trust type that is stronger than a revocable trust. The critically important question is: Just how strong does the trust need to be?

MEET KAREN AND NEAL

Karen and Neal were the successful owners of three hair salons and the proud parents of three adult children, Erin, Colleen, and Sean. Karen's recently deceased mother spent the last six years of her life in a nursing home, so Karen witnessed the financial devastation caused by the failure to plan properly. Karen's parents were "old school" and had only simple wills. These wills provided that all assets were to be left to the survivor of the first spouse to die, and that whatever was left upon the death of the second spouse would go to Karen and her sister.

Karen witnessed the systematic depletion of first her parents' bank accounts and then the proceeds of the necessary house sale in order to pay the steep monthly nursing home bills. She was determined not to let history repeat itself. She urged Neal to join her in consulting a lawyer who specialized in asset protection.

Neal was ambivalent. He felt that at 59 and 64 years old, they were way too young to be thinking about wills. He accompanied Karen to the lawyer in order to end the daily discussion about the subject. Neal tried to follow his late father's advice that "a happy wife is a happy life."

The couple explained their situation to attorney Michael Miller. Karen shared her wishes that the assets they were working so hard to save and build would ultimately benefit their children and grandchildren as opposed to a nursing home. Mr.

Miller correctly advised Neal and Karen that they should create a trust which would own the family home and some portion of their savings and other liquid assets. The attorney further advised his new clients that the trust should not be revocable.

If Karen and Neal retained the power to revoke it, then a future possible nursing home could require that they do just that to pay the enormous bills. This made sense and they went ahead with the trust.

A few years after completing their estate planning, tragedy struck. Their son, Sean, went missing from a cruise ship while on his honeymoon with his new bride, Vanessa. After Sean's funeral, Karen made an appointment with Miller to revise their estate planning. Because Sean left no children, she instructed Mr. Miller to revise the documents so that their daughters, Erin and Colleen, would receive what would have been Sean's one-third share of the estate.

After giving Karen his sincere condolences, Mr. Miller advised that the requested change was not possible. "Karen, you must recall our conversation about the trust being irrevocable?" he asked.

"Yes," she replied. "Surely, though, there must be something we can do in light of the tragedy?"

Turns out that this trust was totally irrevocable. Karen and Neal retained no legal ability whatsoever to make any changes to either the trustee (their daughter, Erin) or to the named beneficiaries (Erin, Colleen, and Sean).

There were two possible solutions for Karen and Neal. Neither one of them would be a real help.

Sean's one-third interest in the trust was now legally owned by his estate. If he had made a will before his untimely death, then his named beneficiaries would be entitled to his share. It was a longshot, given the fact that he was only 32 years old. In order to find out, they needed to ask Vanessa for permission to look through Sean's paperwork. Vanessa claimed that she was too depressed to deal with them coming over just yet. She gamely offered to search the apartment for a will and reported back that there was none.

Without a will in place, Karen and Neal's only other legal option would require Vanessa's cooperation. Remember—when we don't have a will, our state of residence has a default will for us. This statutory formula, in the absence of a legitimate will, provides that a surviving spouse is the sole beneficiary (when there are no children). Vanessa was now the legal beneficiary of Sean's interest in his parent's estate. They didn't know Vanessa that well, having only met her a handful of times. Surely, though, if they explained the problem, she would cooperate and sign her technical interest in the estate over to Erin and Colleen. Right?

Karen and Neal invited Vanessa to the house for coffee. They broke the ice by showing the young widow baby pictures of Sean. They then explained the whole situation, and asked if Vanessa would be willing to accompany Neal and Karen to their attorney's office to sign a few papers and straighten everything out. She appeared to be understanding and told them that she would sleep on it and get back to them. When Karen and Neal hadn't heard anything for more than a week, they called her. They left several unreturned messages.

Perhaps it was too painful for her to be in contact with them. On attorney Miller's advice, they sent Vanessa a document whereby she could waive or renounce her interest in Sean's estate.

They heard nothing for two weeks, then received a letter from Vanessa's new attorney. His client would not be waiving any rights to her beloved husband's estate. The tragic loss left her too emotionally unstable to work. She would require all assets to which she was legally entitled. Miller correctly advised Karen and Neal that Vanessa was angling for a monetary settlement to walk away. She was requesting $400,000, which was the actuarial future interest in Sean's one-third of the estate. Mr. Miller advised that a sympathetic court could very well give this to Vanessa. Then they would be out not only the $400,000 but also significant legal fees. Their best option, he counseled, would be to try to settle the matter. Instead of billing Karen and Neal hourly, as he had done with the estate planning, he offered to take the matter on a "contingency" fee basis. Since Vanessa was legally entitled to $400,000, the attorney fees would be calculated at one-third of whatever reduction he could negotiate from that amount.

Surprisingly, Vanessa accepted their first offer of $100,000. Attorney Miller was also now entitled to $100,000. This legal fee represents one-third of the amount saved ($300,000) from the initial demand of $400,000 and the final settlement of $100,000.

Do you think the attorney deserved this legal fee? In a vacuum, I would say that reasonable minds can disagree. This negotiation was not, however, in a vacuum. Attorney Miller was compensated very handsomely to partially remedy a situation that was his fault.

Of course, the tragic loss of Sean from the cruise ship was the immediate cause of the impasse with Vanessa. Rewinding the sequence of events a bit further, though, exposes some very sloppy legal work.

When Karen and Neal first consulted with Mr. Miller, their stated objective was to protect the house from nursing home claims and also avoid probate for their children. Mr. Miller correctly recognized that a revocable trust would only achieve one of these objectives. He knew that in order to achieve both, a stronger trust was necessary. The problem is that the trust he created was *too* strong.

Between a totally revocable trust and a totally irrevocable trust, there are dozens of great possibilities. The art form of trust drafting is to achieve the right balance between strength and flexibility for a given client. For Karen and Neal, a *totally* irrevocable trust was *totally* unnecessary. Because they had no estate tax exposure (visit mylawyerann.com for the current tax thresholds), the trust could and should have been drafted with greater flexibility.

I would have drafted their trust to allow them to remove and replace the named trustee (Erin), I would have provided that they had exclusive ownership rights to their home during life and most importantly, I would have given Karen and Neal the ability to make changes to the originally named beneficiaries.

Whenever possible, I like the trust creator(s) to retain what's called a "special power of appointment" (SPA). The exact wording will depend on a client's specific situation. One version would be: "The Grantors retain the ability to reallocate the remainder interest between and amongst their lineal descendants and trusts for their benefit only."

This wonderful device accomplishes several things. First, from a psychological standpoint, it affirms that the grantor is still the parent, with the luxury of disinheriting someone. A more concrete benefit of this power has to do with taxes. If we name Erin, Colleen, and Sean as the ultimate beneficiaries, but retain the ability to change this (by way of the SPA), have I made a "completed gift" when I transfer the house and other assets into this trust? The answer is no.

This gives us a few advantages. First, because the transfer into the trust is not a completed gift, I am not required to file a gift tax return. A gift tax return is required to be filed for all completed gifts in excess of the applicable annual exclusion (currently $19,000). Next, retaining the SPA protects trust assets from the beneficiaries' liabilities during the grantor's life. Absent the SPA, the gift into the trust is complete, because I have no retained ability to make changes. Therefore, if one of the three named beneficiaries has a car accident, a malpractice suit, or a divorce, their creditors can and will put a lien on their future interest in the trust assets. Without the SPA, the named beneficiaries' interests have vested, making them fair game for the kids' lawsuits.

In Karen and Neal's case, retaining an SPA would have saved them $200,000! It would have enabled them, upon learning of Sean's death, to reallocate his interest between the remaining named beneficiaries (Erin and Colleen).

So, no, I don't think attorney Miller deserved to be paid $100,000 (plus the fees for the original estate planning) for partially solving a problem of his own making. The sad fact is that he likely didn't know any better. Hopefully, for him, his legal malpractice insurance is up to date.

> The SPA also protects trust assets in another respect. Let's say Karen had died instead of Sean. What would happen to the house if Neal remarried, and his new wife badgered him to add her name to the deed? If the SPA is properly drafted, he won't be able to. Recall that the language allows changes to be made as between the grantors' "lineal descendants and trusts for their benefit only." The word *only* blocks future possible spouses and "special friends" from having legal ownership and possibly then transferring property to their own children.
>
> As if all of these benefits weren't enough, the SPA, under current law, allows the ultimate beneficiaries to escape capital gains taxes upon my death. Recall the six-figure hit that Fred's children will face because he made a completed gift of the house to them during his life.

Retaining the ability to change beneficiaries is one of the ways we prevent a trust from being totally irrevocable. Here are some other powers that the trust creator can retain:

I can retain one hundred percent of the use and occupancy rights to the property. In fact, this last power will be necessary in many jurisdictions, in order to retain veteran's and other applicable property tax exemptions. I can and also should curb my named trustee's powers. I can do this by stipulating that during my life, the property can be sold—but only with my written permission.

Another important retained power is the right to continue receiving all income generated by trust assets. This can be real estate rental income or dividend and interest income generated by liquid assets held by the trust. Retaining the right to receive income produced by trust assets enables the trust to qualify as a so-called grantor trust under the Internal Revenue Code (sections 671 et. seq.). A grantor trust is disregarded for all income tax matters.

A grantor trust allows the creator to continue depreciating real estate and applying the resulting tax deductions on their personal income tax return. Similarly, the trust creator can continue to deduct mortgage interest paid to banks as well as any other expenses properly deductible in the absence of the trust. Under current law, one of the most significant tax benefits preserved by this trust with retained powers (which would be lost with a purely irrevocable trust or outright gift of the property) is the "step-up in basis" on assets passing from the trust to the named beneficiaries, upon the death of the creator.

Currently codified in Sec. 1014 of the Internal Revenue Code (IRC), this provision provides the new owners of appreciated assets with a cost basis equal to whatever the fair market value is at the time of the donor's death, provided that the asset "passed at death" and not before. The following concrete example will stop the head spins:

What are the tax implications if we sell the home from the trust during the grantor's life? In this case, the trust neither helps nor hurts us. The trust creator is still entitled to his or her IRC Sec. 121 capital gains tax exemption of $250,000 ($500,000 for a couple).

The grantor trust enables the creator to basically continue his or her life as normal. All otherwise applicable tax liabilities and benefits can continue to be picked up on the trust creator's individual (Form 1040) tax return. This usually obviates the need for the trust to do its own income tax return. Note that we may later wish to change this if the trust creator requires extended long-term care and we wish to shield the trust income as well as the underlying trust assets. This is yet another reason to create legal structures with inherent flexibility with which to make future needed adjustments.

A logical question at this point, would be: "If I can retain all of these wonderful powers with the trust you describe, how is this trust structure any different from a revocable trust, which you keep telling me, Ann, doesn't properly protect my home?"

If that is your question, may I say that it is an excellent one! Again, the art form or balancing act in trust drafting is to retain the maximum number of powers without causing the trust to tip into the non-protective revocable camp. At its essence, we do this in two ways:

1. We name a person, people, or entity, other than ourselves, as the trustee(s). There can be no asset protection if I am my own trustee. Remember, if I, acting alone, can get my hot little hands on the trust asset whenever I wish, then so can my nursing home and other creditors!
2. The trust requires both the creator's and trustee's signatures in order to sell the property or remove it from the trust. This enables me, in the future, to be able to legally and honestly tell a person trying to sue me, that I (acting alone) have no ability to pluck the house (or other assets) out of the trust, in order to pay whoever happens to be suing me. My named trustee, in this case, will have their arms crossed over their chest and shake their head no.

Playing devil's advocate, though, what if I really want the trustee's signature because I want to sell the house, and he or she refuses? Or what if they are simply on an extended vacation and won't be available for the closing? Recall that we retained the power to remove and replace our trustee, for any reason, or no reason, at any time. I could, for example, put my next-door neighbor in there as trustee for five minutes in order to get my required signature.

It is at this point that I feel compelled to stress that *I am not giving anyone individual tax advice here.* I am simply introducing concepts for your consideration. The application of these ideas will depend upon one's individual circumstances. It is also important to remember that tax laws on the federal and state level change periodically. You are encouraged to use the points I am presenting here to determine whether or not a given lawyer is a pinhead. If you bring any of these topics up, and your lawyer looks baffled, it may be time for a new lawyer. If you are looking for a new lawyer, I am always happy to let you know if I have a good recommendation in your area. I keep and continuously edit a nationwide list.

I have hopefully convinced you of the advisability of considering a trust. A related and logical question, then, is whether we still need a will?

My mantra is that we should all have a good will, but the goal is to not have to use it. The laws of most states provide that some post-death functions can only be carried out by a duly appointed executor of one's will.

Litigation is an example of this. Let's say that the reason for my death is that the hospital dropped me on my head, while moving me from the operating table. In the likely event that my family would want to sue those responsible, they will need to have an estate representative appointed by the court. This should be the executor of a will. Failure to have a will does not mean that the family can't commence litigation. They would, however, need to endure the much longer and costlier administration process, whereby a court appoints an administrator who can then commence litigation.

When Should We Revise Our Planning?

Neither a will nor a trust should be "one and done." We should periodically review and possibly modify our planning based on changes in law, health issues, marital status, and family dynamics. The actor Heath Ledger, for example, had a will but failed to update it after having a child. His will left everything to his parents and sisters.

The bottom line is that we should all have a will, and review it after major life events, such as illness, birth, marriage, and divorce.

TAKEAWAYS

- Joint ownership with rights of survivorship will always trump the provisions of a will.
- A revocable trust will avoid probate but will not confer any asset protection over the assets it holds.
- A totally irrevocable trust is as rotten as it sounds and should be avoided at all costs.
- A trust that lies somewhere in between these extremes is where most of us should be.
- A trust that is strong enough to protect us but also flexible enough to enable us to deal with life's curveballs is our ultimate goal.

4

The Laws of Love and Money

A prenuptial agreement (prenup) may be one of the most important things we can do to ensure our future financial security. It is also the legal document that you are least likely to have.

My client, Kevin, got married last year. He did not for a moment consider getting a prenup. He told me that they were unromantic. He was marrying a "mail order" bride, but a prenup is unromantic!?!

Kevin met the lovely Olga through an "elite" matchmaking program geared toward wealthy men. The process employed by the overseas agency was to send prospective brides to Kevin for six-week "dates." During this time, the young women lived with him and tried to make themselves indispensable. The purported goal of the "dates" was to facilitate an exchange of ideals and aspirations, thereby determining the compatibility of the couple. I'm not sure how many deep conversations were possible, given the participants' language barriers, but somehow, Kevin determined that the first two applicants were not for him. The lovely Olga, however, was a match! That is, until they married.

As of this writing, the couple is still married, but things are not going well. As Olga's English improved, their relationship suffered. Perhaps they were happier not knowing what the other was saying. Kevin came into my office last week with his mother. Kevin is a partner in several restaurant businesses with his mother and other family members.

They wanted assurances from me that Olga would have no claim on the family businesses in the event of a split. Unfortunately, and as you likely guessed, I could provide no such assurances.

There is a pervasive thought out there that assets you come into the marriage with are off limits in a divorce—even without a prenup. This isn't exactly so simple.

Most states in the United States are "equitable distribution" as opposed to "community property" states. That means that a judge has pretty broad discretion to put his or her finger on the scales of justice to bring about a property division that comports with his or her sense of fairness or equity.

As applied to Kevin's situation, this means that all bets are off. Olga can make any number of claims. She may, for example, allege that her indispensable work around the house enabled Kevin to focus on the businesses, thereby increasing their profitability and value. At a minimum, the businesses will be disrupted through a court-ordered valuation process. Forensic accountants may descend upon the restaurants.

I get the distinct impression that Kevin is not eager for the profit-and-loss statements generated by these accountants to be in the same zip code as his income tax returns. The bottom line here is that Kevin will likely offer Olga a significant financial settlement to avoid a protracted court-ordered property distribution.

I was truly curious and asked Kevin why he rejected the notion of a prenup reflexively when I suggested it before the marriage. He told me that it is frowned upon in his culture. It would be considered unromantic and insulting to suggest it. Hmmm—Kevin was an "all in" patron of what seemed to me, a glorified prostitution ring, but a prenup was unromantic?

How to Convince Loved Ones to Get a Prenup

Kevin's mother told me that she urged him to get a prenup before his marriage to Olga. How might her efforts have been successful? The overwhelming majority of my clients tell me that they want their adult children to get prenups prior to marriage. The obstacle, of course, is the fact that adult children are free to do whatever they want—including make bad decisions. Given the fact that Kevin knew at the outset that he probably should have had one, it might not have taken too much effort on his mother's part if her approach had been different.

The problem here was not that Kevin didn't want a prenup. The problem was that he didn't want to be the one asking Olga to sign one. He would have been delighted to be able to outsource this function in order to blame someone else. In this case, Kevin's mother should have redone her own estate planning.

Kevin is an only child and currently the sole beneficiary of all of his mother's considerable assets. What if we redid her beneficiary designations within her will and trust to read: "The remainder beneficiary of all distributable assets, upon my death, is my son Kevin, on the condition that he enter into a prenuptial or postnuptial agreement, as the case may be, which serves to keep assets inherited from me separate from assets that he may choose to comingle with another person."

If that feels too harsh for you, here is a gentler option: "The remainder beneficiary of all distributable assets, upon my death, is my son Kevin, with the hope that he enter into a prenuptial or postnuptial agreement, as the case may be, which serves to keep assets inherited from me separate from assets that he may choose to comingle with another person. My intention being that assets originating with me and my beloved late husband, ultimately inure to the benefit of our lineal descendants." Who can begrudge a grandmother's desire to benefit her grandchildren?

Wait a minute, you may ask, aren't inherited assets already separate property not subject to equitable distribution in a divorce? Technically, the answer is yes. If you are ever asked on a game show, this is the correct answer. In a real-life courtroom, however, things are rarely so black and white.

Olga may have, for example, successfully convinced Kevin to add her name to the inherited assets. Alternatively, her attorney in a future possible divorce case may argue that Olga's efforts improved the value of the properties. Did she, for example, add window boxes and plant geraniums to enhance the curb appeal of real estate? This is known as "sweat equity." Or was a property tax payment made by Kevin from a joint account with Olga's name on it? These are just a few examples of arguments that can be made with the intention of dragging out the divorce proceeding, with the likely aim of securing a larger property settlement.

Much litigation, drama, and trauma can be avoided if parents add the requirement or recommendation of a prenuptial or postnuptial agreement to the distribution scheme within their estate-planning documents. With this in place, the Kevins out there don't have to have a backbone. They can point out the technical requirement within their parent's estate planning documents. Anger can be directed at the parents and/or the estate planning attorney.

Anna and Sal Thought a Prenup Was Unromantic

Anna and her family have owned a popular bagel shop in Northeast Queens for decades. When I first ran for elected office, they were one of only a handful of businesses that allowed me to place a campaign poster in their storefront window. My gratitude would be everlasting. The family was not a law client of mine. I think they preferred to stay with their Italian-speaking attorney. This attorney must have agreed with Anna and her then fiancé, Sal, that prenuptial agreements are unromantic. Perhaps he didn't even think to suggest one. If that is the case, I hope that the limits of his legal malpractice insurance are adequate.

Five years into the marriage, Sal discovered that Anna was having an affair. She admitted that she was in love with their mutual friend, Rocco, and wanted a divorce. The couple was barely afloat financially. They lived in one half of a two-family house owned by Anna's parents. Anna's parents were always cautious when it came to Sal. He came to the marriage with neither money nor a job. Anna's parents were careful not to add his name to the real estate or business. With no children and no assets to speak of, one would think that this would be a quick and straightforward divorce process. Think again.

Sal consulted with a very good attorney, who made a bold suggestion. He advised Sal to make a claim on the bagel business, which was started by Anna's grandparents and run by her family for decades. The argument was that the value of the business was increased by Sal's efforts and addition of new menu items. The court ordered an appraisal of the business.

This process unleashed a top-to-bottom investigation of the business's revenue, inventory, and management practices. Anna's parents produced the income tax returns for the business, which was owned by a corporation (supposedly to guard against liability). The returns showed a very modest annual profit. The business appraiser matched up the reported income with the supply orders. Either someone consistently ordered way too much flour every month, or not all of the sales numbers found their way onto the corporate income tax return. Anna's family was in the hot seat.

To make matters worse, the business showed two W2 (on the books) employees. However, the appraiser noted that there were five employees working in the shop. At about this time, Anna's father, Pasquale, came into my office. He was on the verge of tears. He told me that he did have employees that he paid "off the books" because they refused to accept anything other than cash wages.

The only lawyering to be done at this point was to minimize the damage. Anna's family could not take the chance that Sal would report what he knew to the IRS and New York State Department of Labor. The family ended up taking a big mortgage against their real estate in order to enter into a settlement agreement with Sal. The matter was then taken off the court docket and everyone went on with their lives.

The moral of this story is that when you are in business with other people involved, it is very selfish not to do a prenup. Your decision here has a 43 percent chance of hurting your partners.

I believe that every corporate governance document—whether a shareholder's agreement and bylaws for a corporation, a partnership agreement, or an operating agreement for an LLC—should require all shareholders, partners, or members, as the case may be, to enter into relationship agreements. These agreements can take the form of prenuptial, postnuptial, or cohabitation agreements, depending upon individual situations. The required provision within the applicable relationship documents is that "Acme Widget Enterprises" shall remain separate property and not subject to division or valuation. Note that in equitable distribution states, identifying and agreeing upon what constitutes separate property is not enough.

If, for example, my husband has nothing and I have $500,000 in liquid assets and an interest in a closely held business worth $500,000, a simple prenup keeping the business out of any property division does nothing to guard against the judge considering the property, and ordering that my soon-to-be ex receive a healthy amount of my other assets to compensate for what is in the off limits column. Again, the language in the relationship agreement should prohibit any information about the business from entering the marital dissolution proceeding.

The requirement for a relationship agreement within corporate governance documents is a wonderful way to take the burden off the party reluctant to broach the topic. This obviates their need for a backbone. They can simply point to the written requirement and explain that his or her hands are tied.

A Good Prenup Gives Security to Both Parties

One of the biggest misconceptions out there is that a prenup only favors the wealthier party. If this is true, then it is a very bad prenup.

As with all of our asset-protection legal documents, this should not be a one-size-fits-all proposition. Before finalizing such a document, each party must separately assess their future possible exposure to risk and attempt within the document to minimize or eliminate this exposure.

Consider the case of Jennifer and Frank. He was a 72-year-old, wealthy widower with two adult daughters. She was a 58-year-old, soon-to-be-retired receptionist. They met at the health club where she worked. When they decided to get married, Frank's daughters were adamant that he have a prenup. They didn't trust Jennifer and were concerned that her trip to the altar was motivated by the hope of a payday.

Frank was ambivalent. He assured his daughters that they would always be well provided for in his will. He did, after all, have sufficient wealth to go around. Jennifer was on high alert that she might be asked to "give away her rights" in a prenup. All of her friends warned her that he would definitely get her to sign one. Jennifer was pleased and relieved that he never brought the subject up. She felt that she dodged a bullet.

Frank's daughters were wrong about Jennifer. She was not motivated by greed. She and Frank were very happy. Frank covered all of their expenses. He also voluntarily added her name to the deed of his house as well as to a money market account.

Everything was great, until Frank developed ALS. Jennifer cared for him at home as long as she could. Once it got to the point where Frank required help with all custodial activities, such as feeding, bathing, dressing, and toileting, Jennifer cried uncle. His daughters were in agreement that he required a higher level of care than could be provided at home.

After considerable research, they selected a nursing facility. Frank's daughters, Ellen and Gayle, signed the admission paperwork as Frank's power of attorney. The monthly cost was more than $15,000.

Jennifer soon learned that Frank's Medicare and supplement policy only paid for the first 100 days. Because Frank did not have a long-term care insurance policy in place, he was required to privately pay the $15,000 per month bill once his Medicare coverage of 100 days had been exhausted.

At this juncture, Jennifer consulted with an elder-law attorney. On the recommendation of her friends, she wanted to learn about legal financial protections for the so-called well spouse. The attorney incorrectly advised Jennifer that she would have had to transfer assets to her name alone five or more years ago.

Note that this "five-year" requirement actually only applies to third parties—not spouses. Based on this bad advice, she used the money in their joint account to pay the hefty monthly nursing home bills. When the account was down to exhaust fumes, Jennifer called Ellen and Gayle to ask that they release Frank's other funds, over which they held shared power of attorney. Their response was the beginning of the end for Jennifer.

The daughters told her that there were no accounts remaining in Frank's name. They further advised that upon Frank's diagnosis, he urged them to transfer his accounts to themselves! There was no money left in Frank's name and the daughters refused to pay their father's nursing facility bills.

Jennifer was thunderstruck. Her first priority was to ensure that Frank's care continue uninterrupted. She recalled the attorney's advice that when Frank had spent down all of his assets, they could apply for Medicaid to cover the cost of care. The social workers at the nursing home began the Medicaid application process. Their examination of the required bank statements showed the very large transfers to the daughters within the past five years.

Jennifer explained the treacherous actions of Ellen and Gayle. Surely, Frank wouldn't be penalized for acts committed by others. The caseworker was sympathetic. She told Jennifer that she might wish to press charges against the daughters for stealing money from their father.

Jennifer now consulted with another attorney to assess whether she would be better off suing the daughters in civil court or whether she should go to the district attorney to commence a criminal proceeding.

The attorney briefly summarized the difference in the two strategies before dismissing both of them. Because the daughters made the transfers by virtue of Frank's power of attorney, which he executed long before he had any type of cognitive decline, and because the instrument expressly authorized gifting, the daughters had done nothing wrong legally.

Jennifer's only real option at this point was to try to pull cash out of the house in order to pay the nursing facility bills. Frank's daughters reluctantly agreed to sign a reverse mortgage application on their father's behalf via the power of attorney. Remember that this asset was jointly owned with Jennifer. Therefore, upon Frank's future death, the entire ownership would go to Jennifer. The mortgage, consequently, would not reduce any value otherwise going to Ellen and Gayle.

Jennifer was able to borrow $350,000 from the house. This money together with Frank's monthly pension and Social Security should be sufficient to privately pay for Frank's care through the penalty engendered by the gifts to Ellen and Gayle within the so-called five-year lookback.

This leaves Jennifer in the enormous house, trying to pay property taxes, insurance, and all other expenses from her receptionist salary. Retirement is now out of the question. What a disaster!

WHAT COULD JENNIFER HAVE DONE DIFFERENTLY?

The surprising answer is that Jennifer should have been the one to insist upon a prenup. Again, one of the goals of a good prenup is to safeguard the parties from foreseeable future financial security risks, presented by the marriage. Jennifer and her well-intentioned friends thought she dodged a bullet when Frank did not insist on a prenup. Had they been at my conference room table, I would have strongly recommended one.

Given the considerable age difference between the parties, I would have asked Frank what plans he had in place for future possible long-term care needs. One of the many legal obligations arising from the marital state is a duty to cover the cost of each other's nursing home and other long-term care needs. Under English common law this was referred to as the "Doctrine of Necessaries." Now embodied in statute (written laws), all 50 states require spouses to cover each other's long-term care expenses. Jennifer was probably unaware of this.

Again, ignorance of the law will get you steamrolled! If Jennifer knew she'd possibly be on the hook to cover needed care, she may have been properly motivated to insist that the prenup demonstrate the existence of long-term care insurance or some other concrete plan to pay for future possible needed care. Given that an estimated 40 percent of us will need some type of assistance with custodial care (if we are lucky enough to live that long) and given the fact that spouses are legally responsible to cover each other's costs, it would be foolish not to address the topic within the prenup.

Jennifer learned the hard way that just because one party has more wealth doesn't mean that the other has no need for the protections of a prenup.

The less wealthy party, arguably, has the greater need for legal protections. If, for example, I am living in a home owned entirely by my spouse, I don't want to fear possible homelessness every time we have an argument. A good prenup will establish a baseline level of security for each party.

How can the prenup guard against my not having a roof over my head if my husband is adamant about his family's home of seventy-five years remaining in his name? One option would be for him to provide me with the amount of money reasonably needed to make other living arrangements. Alternatively, the prenup can provide that I be permitted to continue to reside in the home for a period of six months following the divorce.

Both people can be secure in the knowledge that no matter what happens in the future, their basic security will not be upended at any time. With survival fears legally minimized, both parties will likely be happier within the marriage. How is a prenup a bad thing, again?

Second (and Subsequent) Marriages

If there is any cohort of the population for whom a prenup should be a no-brainer, it is those embarking upon a second marriage. The divorce rate for second, third, and subsequent marriages exceeds 60 percent! Those in second marriages are also older, with fewer working years left to recover from a financially ruinous "gray divorce." Further complicating matters is the probability that the parties have children from prior relationships. If I've learned anything from my 20,000+ clients, it is that the adult children of older newlyweds tend not to like each other. For anyone not in a coma, the need for a prenup here should be crystal clear.

MEET KATHY AND PETE

Pete was a 66-year-old retired widower with no children. He met 67-year-old Kathy at a widows and widowers support group run by his church. They hit it off nicely. They discovered an easy camaraderie and shared love of silent movies, bingo, and Scrabble. Their frequent homemade meals sometimes included Kathy's adult daughter, Evelyn. Pete, who never had children, enjoyed witnessing the close relationship between the mother and daughter.

Pete was more than financially stable. He enjoyed a very healthy pension as a retired New York City firefighter. He was also the beneficiary of his late wife's substantial insurance policies. He enjoyed his life but was careful to live well within his means. He used to say that he could afford to stay in the most expensive hotels in the world—as long as he didn't stay too long.

Kathy was still working as a dogwalker. She credited this activity for keeping her in admirable physical shape. She had her own home and a late model hybrid car, and like Pete, she was financially stable.

When they married, in a low-key affair before a justice of the peace, the need for a prenup could not have been further from their minds. Turns out that the document would have been a pretty good idea.

Shortly after the marriage, Kathy sold her condo and moved in with Pete. They kept their finances separate and Pete continued paying all household bills. When Kathy's daughter, Evelyn, announced her impending divorce, it was Pete who offered her and her two teenaged sons his spare bedroom until she was back on her feet.

This was two years ago. Pete's dreams of quiet games of Scrabble are far in his rearview mirror. Instead, he can't escape the seemingly nonstop shouting that the teenagers' *Fortnight* and *Grand Theft Auto* games elicit. He has tried to gently broach the subject of Evelyn making other arrangements. Kathy is sympathetic to Pete's frustration.

The problem is that Evelyn is heavily in debt. She can't afford to even rent an apartment. Kathy confessed that she is dead broke, and therefore, unable to help her daughter.

"What about the proceeds of the condo you sold?" asked Pete.

Evelyn told him that it had been heavily mortgaged because she has been supporting Evelyn and her kids for at least fifteen years. What little profit she walked away with was used to pay legal fees for what turned out to be Evelyn's third divorce.

Pete now has a very difficult decision to make. He can either cough up the money to establish Evelyn and the kids in a new apartment, with no end in sight for his financial obligations. Or he can risk losing Kathy by demanding that Evelyn move out and be forced to make her own way in the world for once.

A well-thought-through prenup could have avoided this heartbreaking impasse.

A Prenup Can and Should Be Used to Address Foreseeable Problems

It drives me crazy when people reject the notion of a prenup because they don't want to focus on divorce before the marriage has even started. If you remember nothing else from this chapter, please keep in mind that a good prenup can set the stage for a smooth, responsible, and drama-free relationship. The provisions of a good prenup will confer security and harmony to an intact marriage.

Sometimes clients tell me things like, "We have decided to keep our finances separate, so I don't feel comfortable asking him about his money."

WHAT!?!? Ladies and gentlemen, the marital state brings with it more than a thousand legal rights and responsibilities. We saw in the Jennifer and Frank saga that spouses are financially responsible for each other's long-term and other health care costs. This is just the tip of the iceberg.

The above-referenced "Doctrine of Necessaries" holds that spouses are legally responsible for each other's basic expenses. Hundreds of years ago, this principle ensured that merchants wouldn't be left on the hook for extending credit to a woman for purchasing livestock, fabric, or skeins of wool. In recent decades, the concept has been extended to vacations and fur coats. It is vitally important that couples familiarize themselves with their partner's financial life before the wedding. This includes a general sense of their spending and saving habits as well as their current level of indebtedness.

How can people say that this is none of their business, when the debt will become their legal responsibility once vows have been exchanged? If you are the party in debt, don't you want to do what you can to shield your partner from it to the greatest extent possible?

The prenup can and should serve to protect both parties from negative outcomes. This should include holding each other harmless for debts. If your spouse has an abysmal credit score, this will pull your new combined household score down. This, in turn, means that your interest rates on mortgages and car loans will be higher. Isn't this something you want to know about?

Part of doing a prenup should include running credit reports. There may be perfectly understandable—even admiration-worthy—reasons for a less than stellar credit score. Perhaps my fiancé maxed out his credit cards to help a relative pay for needed medical care. If so, we can deal with this as a couple, in a proactive, "roll up our sleeves" spirit.

If, on the other hand, I am about to marry a spendthrift, then we should endeavor to erect some legal guardrails between the debts and the other party. This can also be an opportunity for an overspender to reevaluate his or her relationship with money. Prior to the wedding, both partners are likely preparing for a new start. It is very common to implement some healthy living habits in order to embark upon the new chapter from the best possible position. I would be very wise, if, in addition to counting carbs, I find out the exact amounts that my soon-to-be spouse is spending on his vintage car collection. What about the antique typewriter or medieval weapons collection that seemed so charmingly quirky on our first date? I promise that it will become old in a hurry when you learn how much he spends on it.

It would not be unreasonable to create upper limits on such expenditures within the prenup. This will go a long way to reducing arguments over differing spending and savings priorities during the marriage.

Do I have a right to know how much financial help my fiancé is giving his parents, adult children, or maybe an ex because he didn't get a prenup the first time around?

What will this accomplish, other than provoking a fight, you ask? Well, we will have a realistic idea as to how the current level of spending will likely impact our new combined household. As it relates to helping parents, it would be wise to find out whether you live in a state with so-called filial responsibility laws on the books. Nineteen states have laws on the books that hold adult children responsible for parents' expenses—including potentially financially ruinous long-term care expenses! In this uncertain economic environment, it would not surprise me if more states enacted these revenue-generating laws. Please check my website to see where your state stands.

Aside and apart from financial issues, the prenup can be used to address other future possible causes of conflict. Let's say that one party has had difficulties remaining faithful in past relationships. An increasing number of couples are including "infidelity penalties" within their prenups. No, this financial sledgehammer may not stop someone intent on straying. It will, however, ensure that if the cheating results in a split, there will be an extra financial cushion.

Ideally, the prenup can and should be viewed as a security blanket and joint goal-setting device for the couple. After setting limits on perceived frivolous spending, for example, the document should then address the couple's shared financial aspirations, such as a vacation or investment property.

In my practice, I find that my Gen Z clients are far more likely to ask for a prenup than my more mature clients. I think this is a natural outgrowth of their tendency to customize every aspect of life. I asked a 30-year-old client what prompted him to set up a prenup. I thought he would say that his parents suggested it. Instead, he astutely observed that he wished to keep strangers out of the marriage. How perceptive!

Without a prenup, third parties, such as your state legislators and judges, get to decide conflicts and responsibilities with one-size-fits-no-one default laws. Many people customize their vows, right? I urge everyone to view the prenup as the written embodiment of the vows with financial safety nets for both partners.

MEET LASZLO AND EVA

Laszlo's family owns several very profitable hotels. They urged him to get a prenup when Laszlo and Eva announced their engagement. Laszlo admits that he knew his parents were right but was paralyzed—every time he tried to bring the topic up with Eva, he chickened out.

As the wedding date approached, Laszlo's mother, Marta, took matters into her own hands. She wanted to shield her son from being the bad guy and told Eva that the family's business governance documents required all members of the business to have prenuptial agreements. Eva was not pleased with this request. However, given the fact that the wedding invitations had already gone out, she agreed to sign the documents Marta's lawyer prepared. As a token of her appreciation and to demonstrate goodwill, Marta gifted Eva a cherished family heirloom, an antique diamond necklace.

The marriage lasted about a year. Marta and Laszlo were so thankful that the prenup was in place. At least they wouldn't have to worry about their family business. When Eva's attorney tried to have the prenup set aside, Laszlo's family thought that she was angrily spinning her wheels,

> to no avail. They were wrong. The prenup was not honored!
>
> What went wrong? First, the document was signed too close to the wedding date. Second, Eva was not represented by a separate attorney. Either one of these factors could have been enough to invalidate the document.

What went wrong here? Some people hear stories about prenups being invalidated and conclude that they shouldn't even bother creating one. After all, why would we want to bring up such a touchy topic, and incur legal fees to boot, if it won't even hold up when needed?

As with any legal protection document, there are right ways and wrong ways to create a prenup. This should not be a DIY job. Nor should it be a job for an attorney who happens to have a template for the document but doesn't really have nuanced experience in creating them. How can you determine whether your attorney knows what he or she is doing? You should not be reticent about asking how many such documents they've done. I'm sure you would have no qualms asking a cardiac surgeon about their experience. You may even want to ask your prospective attorney if he or she knows the following.

THREE SUREFIRE REASONS FOR PRENUPS TO BE TOSSED OUT

1. The document can be invalidated if executed too close to the wedding date. The rationale is that a party may have signed under duress given the immediacy of the wedding. When a new client's wedding is scheduled six weeks or less

away, I do not take the case. Another bright line rule for me is that we shouldn't create the document after wedding invitations have gone out. Here, a party can claim that they would have been publicly humiliated to cancel the wedding, so they signed whatever was asked.

2. The most common reason for a prenup being invalidated is when the two parties share a lawyer. Shared representation is a waste of the paper that the document is printed on. I am all about saving money, but this is not the place to do it. Maybe Eva knew this and maybe she didn't. The cynic in me thinks that some people sign prenups knowing full well that they won't be honored because they did not have separate counsel. Please note that having two lawyers does not mean that there will be double the legal fees. One attorney typically does the bulk of the drafting. The other attorney reviews the document created and may request additions or modifications. I will not undertake representation of someone requesting a prenup if the other party is not separately represented. The attorney representing Laszlo in the above story should hope that their malpractice insurance is in place. In my opinion, it was incumbent upon him to insist that Eva retain separate counsel.
3. The third way out of a prenup is failure to disclose assets. The rationale here is that a party waiving his or her property rights was not properly informed about what he or she was waiving. The prenup should have two "schedules" attached, reflecting the parties' respective assets and liabilities.

Beyond avoiding the foregoing fatal three, there are a few other issues to consider.

Some couples choose to implement sunset provisions on the prenup, or a sliding scale of property distributions based on how long the marriage lasts. Should I walk away with the same property settlement from a marriage that lasted ten days as one that lasted ten years? Probably not. In any event, I strongly recommend that couples reexamine the document every few years or so and consider modifications.

Like all good legal and life planning, this should not be a "one and done" proposition. Changes to a prenup must, of course, be in writing and agreed to by both parties. Any such modifications will, by definition, take place after the marriage has been finalized. Therefore, the new document will take the form of a postnuptial agreement, hereafter called a postnup. We will discuss these in the next section.

If the home or apartment lease is in the name of one party, thought should be given to the length of time the other person has to make other living arrangements after a split, to avoid someone coming home from work to find their belongings strewn across the front lawn! We also want to ensure that there are adequate safeguards built into our wills and trusts to protect our partner upon death. Remember, even if the marriage beats the divorce odds, it will end at death. Without a properly drafted will and trust, I would likely be doing legal battle with my husband's children from a prior marriage, who are also his "heirs at law."

Another area to pay attention to is how we provide for each other during the period that it takes the divorce to be finalized. Most prenups focus only on property distribution upon divorce. Even though every state now has so-called no-fault divorce, we can still expect a months-long proceeding. What are the living arrangements and financial arrangements during this time? If the prenup calls for some form of spousal maintenance (alimony), when do these payments begin? The period between the decision to split and the time that the divorce is finalized, can be expensive, indeed, for the party who has more assets.

Another point deserving of attention involves a spouse who arguably put their career on hold for the sake of the marriage and family. The classic example is a wife who worked and paid all of the expenses to put her husband through medical school. She then gave up her job to focus on children and the home after her husband was established in practice. It is common for her divorce attorney to request a percentage of all future earnings attributable to the degree. The rationale is that she deserves to be paid for her equity in the degree. Beyond this, should the husband be required to pay for her future higher education or vocational training? Ted and Carolyn are the poster children of why we should address vocational training within a prenup.

I met Carolyn on my first day of law school. We were in line waiting for our ID card pictures to be taken. She seemed to be about twenty years older than the rest of the students. The conversation started with what led us to choose a career in law. Her answer shocked me. She was recently divorced from a high-profile person. I had heard of the protracted and acrimonious proceeding before even meeting Carolyn.

She shared with me that they had no prenup. After a twenty-year marriage and three children, Ted humiliated her with a very public episode of infidelity. She adopted a scorched-earth policy. As the three-year divorce proceeding was winding down, and the property settlement was nearly agreed to, Carolyn asked her attorney if there was any possible means to extract a bigger financial settlement. Her attorney advised that as things stood, she was to receive exactly 50 percent of their joint assets and 50 percent of Ted's earnings over the course of the marriage, as well as a few years of spousal maintenance.

However, he said, "We may be able to ask for some type of vocational training, to make up for your twenty-plus years out of the work force. Is there anything you would like to learn to do?"

She took a day to think it over. Soul searching was not part of her decision-making here. She confessed with a smile that the day was spent researching the most expensive post-graduate education programs within a 20-mile radius of her home on Long Island. And so it was, that Carolyn joined 210 twenty-somethings for a very expensive three-year law school education! She is now a successful divorce attorney.

Failure to have a prenup which placed limits on the financial settlement resulted in Ted leaving the marriage with less than half of the assets. Again, most states in the United States are not community property states, which can reliably be expected to result in a 50/50 distribution. In most states, equitable distribution rules allow judges to basically do whatever they wish, in order to achieve their subjective notion of "equity." It is very probable that the judge felt sorry for Carolyn, and therefore, really socked it to Ted.

My goal is to take the stigma out of creating a prenuptial agreement. I advise my clients and audiences to view the document as an extension of our other legal planning and asset protection documents. Embarking upon the marital state carries with it a host of legal obligations and responsibilities between the parties. These new obligations and rights begin immediately upon marriage. Thoughtful people create estate-planning documents to ensure that their new life partner has the right to make medical and possibly financial decisions for us in the event of incapacity. Most people are also happy and willing to take legal steps to ensure the financial security of the other person in the event of death. The prenup should be properly viewed in this context. We are, at a minimum, establishing a financial security "baseline" for both parties, both within the marriage as well as in the case of the unforeseeable, but statistically possible, future break-up.

TAKEAWAYS

- A good prenup will ensure security and prevent arguments from triggering existential crises for the less wealthy party.
- Never share a lawyer or execute the document too close to the wedding.

5

Legal Agreements between Spouses

All married couples can benefit from legal protections. Whether you are happily married, miserable, or somewhere in between, a legal agreement with your spouse can protect both of you from life's curveballs.

Referred to as postnuptial contracts, legal agreements between married couples are most commonly used during periods of marital crisis.

Until relatively recently, spouses who had issues to resolve only had two choices: grin and bear it, or leave. This is because legal contracts between married people were not recognized under common law. Today, married couples in all but a handful of states have the right to contract with each other in order to resolve or prevent a whole host of problems. These documents enable us to protect assets from being lost to litigation in the context of divorce. They can also preserve wealth by allowing couples to establish savings and wealth-building priorities. Increased legal acceptance has resulted in matrimonial attorneys drafting more of these agreements than ever before.

Postnuptial agreements can be used to modify, bolster, or replace a stale or faulty prenup. Say, for example, the prenup was entered into too close to the wedding day. This could potentially render it subject to attack by the party wishing to disavow it. The basis for such a challenge would be that the close proximity to the wedding date caused a party to sign under duress. A postnup can then be used to revise and restate the terms of the prenup and set it upon solid legal ground.

Most often, though, postnups are used in times of marital crisis. When the cheating spouse is groveling for a second chance, the aggrieved party can now ask for more than just his or her word that it won't happen again. Monetary penalties for future indiscretions are commonly incorporated into the document.

In *Love & Money*, I shared the cautionary story of "Ken and Louise." They were referred to me to discuss a possible postnup in the wake of Ken's multiple infidelities. Louise was on the verge of leaving the marriage and grappled with mixed emotions regarding their future. A trip to a marriage counselor provided little help. The counselor basically told Louise that it was her decision as to whether she should stay or leave. However, if she chose to stay, it would not be constructive to continually bring up the most recent incident.

At my conference table, Ken swore to Louise that it would not happen again. He "now realized just how important [she] was to him" and that "this chapter could somehow ultimately result in a stronger and better relationship."

I was proud of my self-restraint for not rolling my eyes when Ken said this. Instead, I asked if he was willing to agree to a penalty provision within the postnup. (Justin Timberlake and Michael Douglas are among those reported to have agreed to such infidelity penalty clauses.) The gist of Ken and Louise's clause was that if either party was unfaithful at any time, and a divorce occurred thereafter, then the aggrieved party would receive 60 percent of the couple's assets.

Ken agreed to the penalty provision. He had it reviewed by a separate attorney, and they both signed. Two years passed, and things improved between them. For Ken's fiftieth birthday, he asked Louise if she would possibly agree to a threesome. This was his life's biggest "bucket list" item. Her initial reluctance was short lived. Louise was an enthusiastic participant and ultimately developed a relationship with the other woman.

Louise eventually left Ken to marry Renee. Ken was devastated. During the divorce, Ken's lawyer tried to enforce the 60 percent penalty clause within the postnup. This didn't work in Ken's favor, however, because he "consented" to the initial relationship with Renee. It therefore did not qualify as "infidelity" as defined by the contract. In fact, the only conduct that qualified as infidelity was Ken's original affair. Because the divorce took place after Ken's infidelity, Louise ended up with 60 percent of the couple's assets. Though she was the victor in this round, I advised her to create a prenup before taking the plunge with Renee.

Postnuptial Agreements for the Happily Married

I encourage all of my married clients to consider creating a postnup to bolster the integrity of their estate planning. This suggestion is universally met with puzzlement. Why on earth would a reasonably happily married couple need a postnup? Because without one, your entire estate plan might unravel.

Vivian and Carlos created wills with me more than ten years ago. Their distribution scheme within the wills was what you might imagine. Upon the death of the first spouse, they each wanted all of the assets to pass to the survivor. Then, upon the death of the surviving spouse, they wanted their assets to be distributed equally to their two children, Carlos Jr. and Tina. Their biggest concern was that they did not want any assets passing "outside of the family" to either of their children's spouses. Instead, they wanted the assets to go from their children directly to grandchildren. They gave me strict instructions that "nothing goes to the in-laws!"

I explained that once their children inherited the assets, they were legally free to do with them as they pleased. This included sharing the assets with their spouses. Vivian and Carlos were adamant about preventing any of their wealth from going to the in-laws. They were only barely on speaking terms with their son-in-law, Vinny. They hadn't spoken to their daughter-in-law, Tanya, in five years. Having prepared wills for more than twenty years, I have come to learn that it is very common for my clients to have issues with their children's spouses. Five years without speaking, though, was pretty severe.

What could have caused this? I felt that it was my job to ask . . . Somewhat ironically, it turned out that the feud erupted over an estate-planning discussion. Shortly after the birth of their first grandchild, Vivian and Carlos suggested that Carlos Jr. and Tanya create wills to name guardians for little Joachim. Tanya informed them that they already created a will shortly before Joachim was born. The will named her parents as the legal guardians of little Joachim in the event that she and Carlos Jr. were to die before his eighteenth birthday.

Vivian was devastated! How could Carlos Jr. have gone along with this? Tanya's parents were so clearly unfit. They practiced what she deemed a "bizarre" religion and were so utterly ignorant that Vivian felt that it should be against the law for them to even vote.

In response to my further questioning, Vivian conceded that she was still on speaking terms with her son. Yes, she was hurt that he agreed to the selection of his wife's parents, but Vivian reasoned that Tanya must have pressured him into it.

"Surely he was subjected to that domineering [expletive]'s control," Vivian hissed. I turned to Carlos, and as if on cue, he dutifully nodded his silent assent.

I again explained that they couldn't prevent Carlos Jr. from sharing his ultimate inheritance with Tanya. That is unless they (Vivian) felt strongly enough that they were willing to legally restrict Carlos Jr.'s access to his one-half of the estate.

And so it was that Vivian instructed me to draft each of their wills as follows: Upon the death of the first spouse, everything goes to the survivor. Upon the second death, whatever is left of the estate goes one-half to Tina and one-half into a trust for Carlos Jr.'s limited lifetime benefit. Their financial advisor, Shari, was named as the trustee for Carlos Jr. The trust dictated that she give him 5 percent of the trust assets each year, and then upon his death, anything left in his trust was to go to Joachim, together with any future possible siblings he may have.

While this might not be the solution most people would come up with, it was clearly what Vivian wanted. She and Carlos definitely took my advice to customize their estate planning based on their individual situation.

One year after the wills were signed, Vivian died in a car accident. I heard that Carlos was in a state of shock. I called and suggested that he come into the office to review his legal planning. He said that he would, but never did.

Five years later, Tina and Carlos Jr. made an appointment with me after their father died. I assumed that the meeting was to discuss probating the will we had drafted years earlier. I was wrong. They showed me a photocopy of a newer will in which Carlos left everything to Shari.

"His financial advisor?" I asked.

"And widow," Tina added.

Tina and Carlos Jr. would have only received the estate if Shari had died first. Given the fact that she was eighteen years younger than Carlos, this was never a very likely scenario.

I thought about Vivian and how fervently she wished for the family's assets to remain with her children and grandchildren. Now, everything was in the hands of a stranger to the family and there was nothing that could be done to correct it.

I thought hard about what went wrong here. I had reached out to Carlos when I heard about Vivian's death. If he had come in, I definitely would have urged him to get a prenup in the event of a subsequent remarriage. I then concluded that Shari could have easily talked him out of doing one, even if I did have a chance to recommend it. I thought back to my meetings with Vivian and Carlos and how she set the agenda and Carlos just seemed to acquiesce to her wishes.

I Have a Postnup

About ten years into my own marriage, my husband Bill asked me where the lightbulbs were kept. After shaking my head for a moment, I suddenly realized that if I die first, Bill would likely be remarried within months. What would happen to our assets? What good is a well-constructed estate plan if a weak-willed surviving spouse can turn it on its head?

It was then that I began suggesting to my clients that all estate plans should include a limited postnuptial agreement. This requires each party to agree that they will enter into a prenuptial agreement prior to any future possible remarriage.

Bill and I have trusts that leave everything to the survivor upon the first death. The trusts then provide that what's left at the second death goes to our children and favorite charities. If Bill, as the surviving spouse, remarries, could he stand up to the new wife, angling to get her hands on all of our jointly accumulated assets?!

He can promise me this won't happen until he is blue in the face. He's a nice guy who doesn't like conflict. I know that he would quickly cave, if pressed by his new squeeze, to put her name on the assets. She could lie to him by saying, of course, she will make sure our kids are protected later. Thanks, Dear, but I'd like to tie this future loose end up now.

As if to illustrate my point that he is a nice guy who doesn't like conflict, Bill willingly agreed to sign the postnup that I created. In this document, we each simply agree to enter into a prenuptial agreement prior to any future marriage to another person. Our agreement specifies that at least 60 percent of our jointly accumulated assets (measured as of the date of the first death) be legally set aside from any property or assets to be comingled with a future spouse. Some of my clients choose to set aside more assets, some less.

Note that these assets are not withheld from the survivor. He is free to spend and use this money as he wishes. Whatever happens to be left, however, of the 60 percent set aside, will, upon his death, be legally earmarked for our children as opposed to his young widow. Now I don't have to worry about her talking him out of getting a prenup or getting herself written into his will. He doesn't have to have a backbone! He can simply blame it on poor old dead me for making him legally commit in advance to acting responsibly.

Creating this limited postnup will also protect against poor decision-making resulting from a future possible cognitive impairment. Nearly 40 percent of us will, one day, develop some dementia-related illness that affects memory and decision-making. This leaves millions of us susceptible to the undue influence of others. In this context, we are thinking about pressure exerted by a future romantic partner. Protections should be established in advance, in order to blunt damaging effects of a future cognitive impairment.

A POSTNUP CAN PROVIDE A FRAMEWORK AND MECHANISM TO WRESTLE YOUR FINANCIAL DEMONS INTO SUBMISSION

Financial pressures and disagreements have long been among the top factors driving couples to breakup. Remember Billy Joel's friends, "Brenda and Eddie," who "started to fight when the money got tight, and they just didn't count on the tears"? Perhaps it was the ill-advised "big water bed that they bought with the bread they had saved for a couple of years" that set them on an unstable financial road.

Today's young couples are even more likely to be suffering from some degree of financial stress. There are many reasons for this. The cost of higher education has exploded in the past twenty years. Young people are borrowing dizzying amounts of money to pay for college degrees. Today's job market, however, does not guarantee that all of the newly minted grads will find gainful employment. In fact, there are more unemployed college graduates today than there are job openings requiring a college degree. The near impossibility of paying off the average student debt of $25,000 when unemployed or underemployed becomes painfully obvious six months after leaving school when the first student loan bills come in. Add credit card debt to this mix (the average cardholder has a balance of $8,000), and we have the fault lines of a financial disaster waiting to happen. This is the unstable foundation on which many newlyweds are building their financial lives together.

The single most important thing that we can do to prevent marital money woes on the front end is to avoid planning a wedding beyond our means. The average cost of a wedding in the United States is in excess of $30,000! This is two-thirds of what the average college graduate (who is lucky enough to be able to find a job) can expect to make in a whole year. Incurring expenses that you cannot comfortably afford will make you feel icky. When all of these bills start rolling in after the honeymoon, it's easy for a couple to end up resenting each other.

As Dr. Phil says, "When money is a problem, then everything else is a problem."

It is challenging, if not impossible, to be happy in your relationship when there are financial pressures that you feel powerless to fix. I am absolutely not saying that we need money to be happy. What I do believe is that we all need to be free of financial pressures in order to feel happy. As a couple, we can't be at our best if one or both partners are depressed or anxious about finances.

Our ability to honestly confront our financial messes and begin to turn things around is turbocharged when we act as a team. The power of two or more people acting together in a spirit of cooperation will produce far greater results than one person acting alone, or both partners doing what they can separately to fix things.

Andrew Carnegie referred to this concept as his "Master Mind." Long before becoming one of the wealthiest people in US history, the immigrant from Scotland worked as a day laborer making very little money. This was before a legally mandated minimum wage. Employers benefited from a glut of new immigrants eager to work. They were, therefore, free to pay laborers next to nothing. During Mr. Carnegie's early working years, his pockets were usually empty, and he barely had enough to eat.

Somehow, even in his humble circumstances, he believed that he was capable of amassing great wealth. He was convinced that the first step in this process was to surround himself with a group of people who had the same objective. He referred to this group of people with shared goals and a cooperative spirit as his "Master Mind" group. They met periodically to brainstorm on creative methods to save from their meager wages and strategically invest their savings. Andrew Carnegie often said that he would never have accomplished his remarkable financial feats had he tried to go it alone.

Modern business leaders employ this principle when assembling teams to attack a problem or come up with new ideas. A spirit of harmonious cooperation between individuals becomes a powerful force. What two or more people can accomplish together is truly greater than the sum of what they could accomplish separately. That is, if they are freed from thoughts of competition between themselves.

Unhealthy competition, comparison, and envy are anathema to productivity. I saw this principle at work as a legislator. In the wake of gripping news stories, dozens of my former colleagues would rush to introduce legislation designed to fix the given problem. Jockeying and arm twisting over who would be the successful "prime sponsor" of the bill was great spectator sport. It occurred to me early in my fourteen years as a legislator that there was no limit to what one could accomplish once we lost concern over who would get the credit. Putting ego to the side and focusing on a great result, can't help but benefit all involved.

"A rising tide lifts all ships." Likewise, constructive and harmonious teamwork benefits all team members.

Why, then, do so many couples refuse to confront their financial problems as a team? Studies show that most of us have some financial secrets from our partners. I refer to this as financial infidelity. These financial secrets, if big enough, can cause misery and erode the fabric of the relationship.

Take the case of Lori and Gregg. He was a successful accountant, and she was a legal secretary. They were active in civic and political circles in my community. We were not especially close, because Gregg was on the other side of my political aisle and actively supported the incumbent that I initially unseated, as well as each of my subsequent political challengers. He was not, however, one of my (many) really mean political adversaries. I admired Gregg and Lori. They seemed genuinely happy and had three beautiful children, a gorgeous house, and many friends. I aspired to what they had during my single girl days.

A few years back, Lori made an appointment for a legal consultation with me. Gregg had a horrible accident and was paralyzed from the chest down. She needed help transferring their joint assets into her name in order to try to protect them from the likely financially ruinous nursing care bills that lay ahead. Gregg and Lori had not purchased long-term care insurance and quickly learned the limitations of their other insurance. Fortunately, Gregg was still able to work as an accountant from home. His income had continued uninterrupted since his accident four years prior.

Lori told me that she had a decent but not perfect handle on the nature and extent of the couple's finances. We agreed to meet again the following week when she was to bring copies of deeds to their home and investment property and financial account statements. The next day, she appeared at my office in tears and pleaded with my scheduler to be squeezed in immediately.

The financial statements she pulled together revealed that the couple was nearly broke. Lori had gladly let Gregg deal with the finances since they were first married. He is, after all, an accountant. It came to light, however, that Gregg had been an unemployed accountant since his accident. For the past four he had been methodically transferring money from their investment accounts into their joint savings in amounts equal to his prior income. The only account balance that Lori ever looked at was the primary joint savings (with linked checking). She saw the weekly additions and had no reason to think anything was wrong.

When Lori angrily confronted Gregg, he broke down. He admitted that he had been let go from his firm shortly after the accident. His initial plan was to live off their investments while he searched for another job that he could do from home. When no such job materialized, he planned to start a private accounting practice. He just didn't want Lori and the kids to worry while he tried to implement a new source of income.

Lori was beside herself. An assessment of their remaining funds revealed less than that needed to cover six more months of their current expenses. She reluctantly decided to sell the four-family investment property that had been in her family for generations. After all, tenants hadn't been paying rent for many months due to the moratorium on evictions during the pandemic.

Fortunately, she found a buyer pretty quickly. It was an all-cash deal, so there were no delays with the buyer seeking a mortgage. The closing date was scheduled. Then her real estate attorney told her that an issue was flagged by the buyer's title company. The property was heavily mortgaged! Yep—Gregg borrowed against the property.

"How could he have done this?" she wailed.

Well, he was able to do this legally because of two mistakes Lori made.

Early on in their marriage Gregg told her he felt like a second-class citizen because the rental property was in Lori's name alone. This was a low-simmering source of contention for some time. After the birth of their second child, Lori reluctantly agreed to add his name to the investment property originally purchased by Lori's grandparents.

Lori's next mistake, in retrospect, was granting Gregg a one-size-fits-all, unlimited power of attorney, whereby he was able to conduct business transactions for her and *sign her name to all documents—including mortgage applications*!

She was legally powerless to do anything about what had happened.

Lori's "power of attorney," which she ordered online seemed like a real bargain at the time. The website seemed legit and guaranteed the legal validity of its documents. They were valid, all right! So much so that Gregg was able to strip most of the value out of her family's property. A good lawyer could easily have placed reasonable limits on the powers granted, depending upon the specific situation. Gregg's powers, for example, could have stopped just short of being able to mortgage or sell real estate.

Lori's bigger mistake was to turn a blind eye to the couple's finances. She confessed that she hadn't opened a bank statement in the past twenty years! She told me that she was never comfortable dealing with or even discussing money. Her willful ignorance in this regard allowed the family to be financially devastated. Now Gregg and Lori's adult children are trying to give them some money until they come up with a plan. According to both of them, the marriage is irretrievably broken. Unfortunately, they can't even contemplate divorce or separate living arrangements because they have no money.

How could a postnuptial agreement have helped? I believe that it would have set the stage and provided a framework for Lori and Gregg each having an active role in the household finances. The exercise of financial goal setting and periodic review embodied in the postnup would have required Lori to look at financial statements periodically. Do you think that this periodic review would have made Gregg more or less likely to go rogue and spend the couple's money wildly?

Financial infidelity can take many forms. I would define it as taking actions that negatively affect both parties' financial life without the other's knowledge. Most of the aggrieved spouses I've interviewed in the wake of a financial infidelity disaster admit to having had a feeling that something was off.

MEET LIZ AND JORDAN

My estate-planning client, Liz, told me she felt like something was wrong with her husband, Jordan. Liz was more than an active participant in the couple's financial dealings. She was the spouse in charge of paying household expenses and monitoring and managing their household finances. All of their finances were on track. It was their relationship that she thought had hit a rough patch. Jordan was a bit remote and withdrawn. He attributed this to his demanding work as the COO of a major investment firm. His extensive travel requirements left him sleep-deprived and edgy.

One morning as Jordan was leaving the house, Liz noticed his keys left on the table. He pulled out of the driveway before she made it outside. She texted him to let him know. He said he didn't need them.

As she placed the keys on Jordan's dresser, she noticed a small post office box key. Hmmmm-they didn't have a PO box. Or did they?

Her field trip to the post office would have to wait an hour until it opened. In the meantime, she did some digging. Nothing unusual in the house.

She felt guilty going through his drawers and closets, sort of. Nothing unusual in the basement or garage either. Now she felt a little more guilty but proceeded to check out the PO box. Fairly sure that this was a wild goose chase, she planned to make Jordan a lovely dinner to compensate for her invasions of his privacy.

Instead of a trip to Whole Foods to buy dinner fixings, though, a call to her divorce attorney was in order. Jordan had an active PO box all right. In it she found a brokerage account statement in his name alone. The balance was near $500,000!

When confronted later that night, Jordan insisted that he had done nothing wrong. He was planning to surprise her with the account. He imagined that they would buy a vacation home with it. Was she now wracked with guilt because of her mistrust? Far from it. She didn't believe a word that came out of his mouth. She apologized to him for both her behavior and inability to shake the feeling that something was way off. Would he be willing to submit to a lie detector test?

Jordan was not willing. He told her that her actions went too far. He was done with their marriage. He filed for divorce. Liz's divorce attorney urged her to engage a forensic accountant to ensure that there were no other hidden accounts. The research didn't turn up any other accounts. They did, however, discover transfers from Jordan's solo account into someone else's account. This prompted the engagement of a private investigator. Turned out that the sanctimonious Jordan, who was so outraged over Liz's lack of trust, was actually engaged to another woman. His plan was to sock away savings that would not be on the radar screen during the property distribution phase of his planned divorce from Liz!

What could Liz have done differently to avoid this horrible result? Well, she could have given some thought to the early days of their relationship. When they first met, Jordan was married to someone else. He swore to Liz that the relationship was beyond over. He was simply waiting it out until his youngest child left for college the following year. He and Liz kept their relationship under the radar, while they planned and saved for their new life together.

Never in a million years did Liz imagine that she would be in the position of Jordan's clueless first wife. Perhaps it was the brain-altering oxytocin emitted early on in a love relationship. Maybe it was Liz's healthy ego. In any event, she found herself now in a position that she never imagined, let alone prepared for.

We would all do well to consider the possibility that we don't always see things objectively. If Liz had been my friend or client when she first met Jordan, I would have begged her to get a prenup. Given Jordan's prior history of infidelity, and given the fact that Liz had substantially less wealth coming into the relationship, she

> should have legally safeguarded her future financial security. She also could have asked for a postnup as Jordan was adamantly denying wrongdoing. Both documents could have contained an infidelity penalty provision, whereby a party who was cheated on gets a bigger settlement upon divorce.

Financial infidelity often takes the form of secret spending. Sometimes, as with Liz and Jordan, we see secret savings. Without question, though, the most damaging form of financial infidelity is secret criminal activity. In these cases, one spouse desperately tries to demonstrate that they knew nothing because the wrongdoing was kept well hidden.

Who believes that Ruth Madoff was unaware of her husband's decades-long criminal Ponzi scheme? Bernie Madoff was unwavering in his insistence that she and their sons had been kept in the dark. The prosecutors in the case did not meet their legal burden to prove that she knew or should have known what was going on. She has, therefore, never spent a day in jail, even though she seems to have benefited for decades from the fruits of the illegal activity.

The claim of innocent spouse is seen most often in the context of fraudulent income tax returns. There have been countless tax fraud cases where one party claims they had absolutely no idea what was on the return. Here, the legal presumption is that both parties who sign the tax return have a decent understanding of its contents. Courts today are generally less likely to believe that anyone is a clueless nitwit unaware of what they are signing. The burden has shifted to the party claiming ignorance to demonstrate how this is possible. We know that ignorance of the law is no excuse. What about ignorance of the facts? Well, that depends . . .

When Michael Meisner was being prosecuted for a $30 million Ponzi scheme, both he and his wife, Victoria, maintained that she knew absolutely nothing about it. Did she know? In the income tax fraud component of the case, Victoria claimed that she did not even look at the tax return she signed. The relevant legal inquiry, however, was not whether she knew, but whether she should have known.

To answer this question, the prosecution looked at the couple's lifestyle and spending patterns and compared them to the amount of income reported to the IRS. In the year prior to Michael's arrest, Victoria had quite the lifestyle, indeed! Evidence adduced at trial consisted of credit card statements showing that she spent $400,000—on one credit card alone! The tiny problem for Victoria was that the income tax return she signed, declared total annual income for the couple of only $40,000. Victoria did some jail time.

A few years back, we saw another claim of "innocent spouse" play out in a New Jersey courtroom. Teresa Giudice, of "Real Housewives" fame, claimed that she had no idea that the couple's joint income was grossly minimized on several federal tax returns. As in the Meisner case, prosecutors in the Giudice trial adduced evidence of a very lavish lifestyle. The prosecution in this case was also able to show that in the same year that Joe and Teresa reported a very small income on their tax return, they showed a very high income on mortgage application documents. The jury didn't buy the couple's attempt to tap dance around the discrepancy. Both parties did jail time.

Do I believe that a postnup could have prevented this criminal behavior? Well, to the extent that a good postnup dealing with financial goals requires the parties to set forth their values and family aspirations, the process may well have recalibrated their thinking. Wealth built on a foundation of lying, cheating, and unfair dealing cannot last.

Remember, a central theme reported by lottery winners and other windfall recipients who lost it all is that they felt unworthy. Those who have a real reason to feel unworthy, because of fraudulent or criminal acts, will act in such a way as to separate themselves from the ill-gotten gains. Lasting wealth can only be built on a foundation of honest and fair dealings.

Healthy Financial Separateness

Some amount of financial separateness is a good thing. I don't want to be obliged to check in with my husband before going out to lunch with a friend. Nor do I really want to see what Bill spent on Valentine's Day flowers on a joint credit card statement.

The question that couples need to answer is what amount of financial separateness works for them. This will depend upon the nature and extent of their assets as well as their personalities. This is ideally hammered out within the financial section of your postnup.

I know that there is visceral pushback to the notion of putting so much detail in writing. Think things will sort of just work out? For the 60+ percent of couples reporting financial stress, the answer is no.

If you are perfectly happy with the current state of your finances, and see that your goals are on track to being met, congratulations. For those who would like different results, you may wish to try a different approach. Doing the same thing cannot help but deliver the same results. I urge couples to at least go through the exercise of creating a postnup to establish spending limits and wealth accumulation goals.

The act of putting things in writing transforms wishes into concrete measurable goals. Putting things in writing guards against differing recollections and expectations. Science shows us that the act of writing helps our brains to better remember things. Going through the written exercise with a partner harnesses the power of Mr. Carnegie's "Master Mind" principle. Two or more people working in unison toward a common goal can unleash creative energies greater than the sum of their individual efforts. Two or more people working cooperatively can and will transform vague wishes into an action plan.

An often-repeated refrain from success coaches is that *what we focus on grows.* There is scientific proof for this notion. Heisenberg's Uncertainty Principle explains the difficulties of scientific measurement in the context of measuring the velocity of electrons. The premise is that it is impossible to accurately measure the velocity of an object because the very act of measurement alters the result. As it relates to a written financial action plan within a postnup, this is a very good thing!

By periodically measuring our results, we are actually bringing about a changed result. The acts of writing and measuring transforms the dabblers trying to wish their dreams into reality into those who create their realities.

TAKEAWAY

A good postnup will ensure that your estate plan is not turned upside down upon your death. It will also create a framework with which you can create, track, and achieve joint financial goals.

6
Protecting Nonrelated Loved Ones

There is a widespread misconception that unmarried couples do not need to be concerned with legal documents and entanglements. Indeed, the desire to keep things simple is at the heart of why many couples choose to remain unmarried. If this is you, I need to tell you that no one needs the protections of solid legal documents more than unmarried couples. Why is that? Among other reasons, if you are in a committed relationship but not married, legal documents will protect you from each other's wacky relatives.

MEET REGGIE AND KRISTIN

Reggie and Kristin were in their mid-forties, and both were survivors of acrimonious divorces. Neither of them wished to take the plunge again. This position was one of their favorite qualities about each other. Several months into their relationship, Kristin's apartment lease was up for renewal. Based in no small part on projected cost savings, they made the decision to live together in Reggie's condo.

Things were going really well for the couple until Reggie became sick, two years into the relationship. The small cough that he attributed to allergies was actually lung cancer. By the time it was diagnosed, it was at stage four and inoperable. The very rapid downhill spiral had Reggie on a ventilator within months. Kristin knew that he would not wish to live if there was no hope for his recovery and his life was reduced to that of mere existence.

After arriving at the difficult and painful decision, Kristin advised the medical team that Reggie should be removed from life support. It was at this point that the legal drama soon rivaled that of the medical. It turned out that Kristin had no legal standing to make any such decision. She was neither a spouse, nor a duly appointed agent under a health care proxy. The hospital would have to contact a family member.

Reggie's estranged sister, Maura, was soon on the scene. She promptly gave the hospital the

OK to remove Reggie from life support. She then insisted on handling the arrangements for the small funeral. Kristin was more than a little relieved when Maura returned to her home, somewhere in New Jersey. Her relief would be short-lived.

As Kristin began to get on with her life, she received a letter from a law firm. It was a notice to vacate the condo, on behalf of their client, Maura, who was the condo's new owner.

Kristin quickly retained her own lawyer and told him that there must be a mistake. Reggie hadn't spoken to his sister for years prior to his illness. He would never have left her the condo. On this last point, Kristin and Maura were in complete agreement. Reggie did not leave Maura the condo. He did not leave it to anyone, because he never got around to doing a will or a trust.

Remember, when we don't decide who gets our stuff by way of a valid will and/or trust, our state of residence has a default plan ready. The so-called intestate laws are an inflexible black-and-white formula that never protects unmarried cohabiting couples. A good cohabitation agreement (cohab) could have addressed many issues, including decision-making in the event of incapacity and inheritance rights for the parties upon death. It is important to point out that the cohab sets forth the nature and scope of legal rights and responsibilities between the couple. They must, then, actually create the necessary advance directives and other documents.

Some jurisdictions have attempted to put a degree of protections in place for domestic partners. These, however, are nowhere near sufficient to properly protect your live-in partner.

Kristin and Reggie's failure to create legal protections for each other resulted in an estranged relative making life and death medical decisions and then inheriting a home and life savings! Even Maura must have been shocked by Reggie's failure to plan.

If you are living with someone, it is critically important that you give some thought to protecting that person in the event that you become incapacitated or die. At a minimum, cohabiting couples need to create: health care proxies, to make each other's medical treatment decisions; powers of attorney, to handle bill paying and other financial transactions in the event of incapacity; and lastly a will and/or trust, to ensure that the surviving party has financial security—and a roof over their head!

I believe that the foregoing advice makes sense to everyone. Failure to deal with these legal protections does not stem from a belief that they aren't needed. If you are in this situation and have not yet protected your live-in partner, I believe the reason is nothing more or less than good old procrastination. You know, logically, that there is a statistical chance of an existential crisis occurring before you get around to taking care of things. You may be willing to accept that chance, because there is also a chance that you will get around to dealing with it before the catastrophe occurs. My sobering message to folks who are willing to kick this proverbial can down the road is that there is real harm in the mere postponement of this planning. Once we know there is something we should do, we will experience some degree of mental discomfort or pressure until we complete the action. This so-called Zeigarnik effect was discovered by researchers. Uncompleted items on our to-do lists cause us to experience very real stress.

This is why removing unnecessary items from this list is liberating. Motivational speaker Dean Graziosi encourages us to work on our "Not-To-Do" lists. Once we've removed some items from our to-do lists, only the most important items will remain.

Creating security for our loved ones should be at the top of the list!

If we know that we should take actions to legally protect loved ones, but have not yet done so, we will feel some stress or guilt each day that we fail to address it. What happens once we address it? The opposite, of course!

Am I actually saying that estate planning will make you happy? Absolutely!

Taking informed action to protect those closest to us results in a feeling of virtuousness. My clients report increased levels of security, self-esteem, and happiness once they've embarked upon the planning process. The good news is that it is very easy (and free) to begin. Please visit my website to download and complete your health care proxy. This will eliminate anxiety and confusion amongst those closest to you in the event that you can't speak for yourself. Once you've completed the document, it is a good idea to take a photo of it with your phone. I also recommend texting it to your named agent, so it will always be readily accessible.

In addition to making provisions for death and incapacity, the cohab should address the brass tacks of who gets what upon breakup. Here, we want to address our existing stuff, as well as create a framework for future possible distribution of items acquired after the date of the cohab.

The "breakup" section of the document must also address post-split living arrangements. If I own the home, we need to specify how long my partner has to clear out belongings and make alternate living arrangements. The stickier issue is whether or not I should be required to give my soon-to-be ex some financial help. Failure to address this within a cohab could well end up in protracted litigation. Every state will entertain a cause of action based on an "implied contract" theory. Was there an understanding between the parties that one would be made financially whole for having contributed uncompensated work, for example, that benefited the other's business or career?

Non-Disclosure Clause

An essential element of all relationship agreements is a mutual promise not to publicly disparage each other. After a breakup, this is an exceedingly tough promise to keep. For thousands of years, the brokenhearted were free to vent with their friends and family in a no-holds-barred manner. Friends would listen dutifully to tales of thoughtlessness and treachery, while copious amounts of alcohol were consumed. Today's technology, though, makes this post-breakup rite of passage downright dangerous. Who among us does not have images or stories of an ex that could cause serious damage to their reputations and, by extension, their careers?

This damaging content is no longer confined to the inner circle of the brokenhearted. Indeed, with the press of a button, the damaging content can, quite literally, make its way around the world. Historically, non-disclosure clauses were limited to the worlds of the uber-famous. Nannies, employees, romantic partners, and partygoers are routinely asked to sign these documents prior to stepping into the inner sanctum of a celebrity. Today, however, we are all just the drunken press of a button away from excruciatingly embarrassing worldwide infamy.

The non-disclosure clause should establish a monetary penalty for violations. At a minimum, the clause should also require both parties to delete any potentially embarrassing photos or videos (ahem) of each other. It can go further to require the destruction of any photo, image, or video of the other party whatsoever. This will prevent someone from claiming that the post was accidental, or that someone else did it.

Marriage Position Clause

It is also a good idea within the cohab to set forth the parties' positions and expectations regarding future possible marriage. What we are seeking to avoid here is a post-breakup claim that marriage was promised. At its essence, this clause will state that there is no present intention to marry, and that no such promises or inducements have been made between the parties.

If I agreed to this in writing, I will be hard-pressed to later claim in court, "I gave him the best years of my life, Your Honor. There was a clear understanding that we would marry once his spousal support payments to his ex-wife were completed."

Can nonmarried people actually pursue such a legal theory in court? In all fifty states, we can absolutely bring a legal action for breaking an implied contract. To successfully press such a claim, I will need to demonstrate that I was induced to suffer some career hardship or forego other opportunities because my ex promised me either marriage or a share in his or her business upon sale.

Engaged couples most definitely need to consider protecting themselves from the financial consequences of a breakup. An engagement elevates the couple's status and consequently expands the theories of legal recovery for a breakup. This is because roughly half of US states still have some version of so-called Heart Balm, or breach of promise to marry, laws in place.

These laws can be traced to medieval times. The theory we ascribe to early versions of these laws is that society wanted to prevent cads and louts from proposing, having their way with a young woman, and then breaking off the engagement. The idea was that a woman's future marriage prospects would be diminished because everyone would suspect that she was no longer a virgin.

Today, a broken engagement can well give rise to a lawsuit. Some 99.9 percent of these suits end in a settlement. This is because courts really do not want these actions proceeding to trial. Judges and their law secretaries (these are attorneys) are notorious for pushing settlements so that the court calendar moves freely.

Having served as a law secretary in the court system, I can tell you how the settlement is accomplished. We would meet with the two parties individually and drill down on the weaknesses in their cases. The clear implication being that the judge was not inclined to agree with their position if they refused settlement and instead proceeded to trial. Indeed, they would be far better off to offer or accept a settlement, we counseled. Each party left the settlement discussion believing that they would be the loser in a trial.

It is during the settlement talk that a party with an absolutely meritless claim will be advised to withdraw it, lest they be hit with sanctions for instituting "frivolous litigation." Through the settlement process, much of our nation's justice is meted out. The overwhelming majority of cases filed in the US do not proceed to trial.

Is this sort of informal process highly subjective? Is it possible for the judges' (and court attorneys') personal feelings to influence the ultimate outcome? Yes and yes. Your goal as a defendant in any type of breakup case is to have a very boring story.

What you don't want is for the judge and court attorney to be shaking their heads behind closed doors about the thoughtless and cruel manner in which you called the relationship off. Consider the story of Terri and Ed that I previously shared in my first book, *Love & Money*.

Terri and Ed dated on and off for two years following Ed's bitter divorce. He did not unequivocally rule out marriage, but he made it clear that it would be a long way down the road. Terri was undaunted. She was sure that if she put the time in and remained patient, Ed would come around. When Terri's apartment lease renewal contained a 20 percent rent hike, she asked Ed if she could crash at his place while she looked for another apartment.

Once in his home, Terri lost no time making herself indispensable. She bought groceries, cleaned, and even cooked occasionally. Terri's new apartment never did materialize. They fell into a comfortable rhythm, punctuated by Terri's occasional marriage references.

One year after moving in, Terri intensified her focus. She told Ed that her Aunt Fran had been diagnosed with macular degeneration. Terri was heartsick that she would be the only woman in her family for whom Aunt Fran would not be able to hand sew a custom wedding gown—that is, unless Ed wouldn't think that it was totally bizarre to have Fran create one for Terri now, before she lost her vision. She joked with Ed that the ultimate wedding might not even feature him, so he shouldn't feel any pressure.

The gown was a masterpiece. Terri showed it to all of their friends, who began asking Ed when they were going to set a date. Though he hadn't technically popped the question, Ed seemed to be objecting less to her marriage program. Over dinner one night, Terri revealed ten index cards with the words "Honeymoon Destination" written across the top. Just for fun, she suggested that they each write their top five destinations and then trade cards to see if there were any matches. Bingo! They each selected Sicily. Though there was still no date (or proposal) in sight, Terri treasured the honeymoon index card with Ed's writing on it.

Convinced that he really wanted her to take the initiative, Terri proceeded to sign up for a bridal registry. When Ed received the confirmation and congratulatory email from the store, he lost it. He immediately began packing up her belongings and putting the boxed items in the hallway.

When Terri and her sister Sharon got home from the mall, Ed told her that he'd had it. Her bizarre little fantasy had succeeded in taking their relationship to an entirely different level, all right. They were now over! Loud enough for the neighbors to hear, Ed yelled that Terri needed psychological help and he would not marry her. His neighbor, Suzy, opened her door to see Ed throw the wedding gown at Terri.

In spite of her broken heart, Terri was determined not to let him get away with treating her so horribly. She met with four separate attorneys who told her that there was no legal remedy available to her. Terri's fifth consultation landed her an attorney who took the case on a contingency fee basis. They proceeded to sue Ed for "breach of promise to marry."

Ed had a good laugh when he was served with the suit. The smile was long gone by the time his attorney told him that his was one of twenty-six states that still had these laws on the books.

"But I never even proposed to her," railed Ed.

After listening to the entire twisted tale, Ed's attorney asked him what the jury would think once they heard that Ed had driven Terri to multiple wedding dress fittings? What about the card, in his writing, selecting their honeymoon destination? What about neighbors who could testify to hearing him "call off the wedding"?

Ed could take his chances with a sympathetic jury, or he could offer Terri $50,000 to drop the case. He paid the $50,000, consoling himself with the (incorrect) notion that he would be able to deduct this payment from his income taxes that year as a gambling loss.

The moral of this cautionary tale is that you can never underestimate the sympathy factor when juries are asked to compensate the lovelorn.

Some examples of how not to break up should be obvious. It is never advisable to break up on social media. Nor should we announce our decision on a post-it note left on a box of Cheerios. Both of these methods have proven costly. The bottom line here is that we should treat our soon-to-be ex with respect, sensitivity, and kindness, whenever possible. Not only is this the right thing to do, but it will also very likely protect you from being served with a costly "Heart Balm" action.

Moreover, by treating our soon-to-be ex with grace, our own feelings of self-esteem will be elevated. This goes a long way toward developing the belief that we are deserving of all good things.

Who Gets Fluffy and Fido?

About 68 percent of US households have pets. Given the fact that 43 percent of married couples will divorce, and over 60 percent of second marriages and unmarried couples will break up, custody of pets is a huge issue. Unfortunately, the vast majority of folks make no arrangements for this on the front end.

An essential component of protecting our assets and our loved ones is the creation of legal safeguards to ensure that our furry loved ones have a smooth transition upon the death or breakup of their "pet parent."

All of the relationship agreements—prenups, postnups, and cohabs—should deal with custody of existing pets as well as future acquired pets. Failure to deal with this yourself will leave the matter to a court. This is usually not the best result for the pet and will likely burn through significant assets in legal fees.

The law in the vast majority of states provides that custody of a pet goes to the party who can demonstrate proof of purchase or adoption. This method utterly fails to take into consideration the reality at the time of the breakup. What if the other party has taken on most of the caregiving and has developed a bond with the pet that is stronger than whoever happened to adopt or purchase her? This default law used by the courts also fails to address a situation where one party acquired the pet as a gift for the other party.

Let's say that my boyfriend adopted a cocker spaniel and surprised me with it five years ago. During this entire time, I have been the one who provides the recreation, affection, and food and coordinates medical care. Even if my boyfriend has been indifferent to the pooch, or only minimally involved, he will be the one who gets custody if we break up! The court is only interested in who acquired the pet.

Why, you may ask, would custody be a contentious issue if my boyfriend doesn't even like the dog? Well, unfortunately, it is very common for angry soon-to-be exes to weaponize pets in order to hurt each other. I have seen people ask for sole custody of the pet and then magnanimously agree to joint custody as a means to force a continued connection with the other party.

As of this writing, there are only a handful of cases where courts have made custody decisions based on the "best interests" of the pet. This is the standard used for determining child custody. Doesn't it make sense to decide this issue on your own? Even if the law evolves to the "best interests" standard across the board, you should want to spare everyone involved the legal fees and drama of a protracted court proceeding.

Again, it is critically important to deal with this issue on the front end.

It is not always possible, though, to know which person will be in the best position to care for a pet, in time to come. Therefore, many couples choose to simply create a framework for deciding custody, in time to come. Who, for example, will likely have more time to spend with the pet? Who has been dealing with primary care up until that time? Whose new living arrangements will afford the pet more opportunities for outdoor recreation? Who will have more financial resources to ensure that primary and preventative medical care is seen to?

The pet custody provision should also provide a dispute resolution mechanism to be used in the absence of a consensus agreement between the parties. We may, for example, agree to arbitration before a retired judge. The general takeaway here is that whatever we can do to stay out of a courtroom is advisable!

TAKEAWAYS

- A good cohabitation agreement will provide both parties with financial and emotional security.
- Create health care proxies, powers of attorney, and trusts to ensure that estranged relatives aren't inheriting your stuff or making life and death health care decisions.

7
The Laws of Creating Wealth

About fifteen years ago, I was invited to give an asset protection seminar to a church group. There was clearly some miscommunication between the person who invited me and my office scheduler who booked the appearance. Upon arrival, I learned that the group all lived in public subsidized housing and had no assets to speak of.

As I waited to be introduced, I knew that my normal presentation focused on protecting assets through trust planning would be tone deaf. Without a plan B in mind, I was introduced as follows: "Our guest speaker for today is Mrs. Ann, and she is here to tell us how to get some assets!"

Wow—after a split second of terror, it occurred to me that I could, in fact, share my own story about how I got some assets!

My husband, Bill, tells me that he envies my poor childhood. He attributes my drive and discipline to my early years of not having what I wanted. Bill did not grow up poor. He tells me of his embarrassment at being dropped off at school in a Rolls Royce. He would ask his mother to drop him off around the block. I can relate to being embarrassed at drop off. In my case, though, it was because of a muffler dragging on the ground, or because the car, at any given time, had different colored fenders.

It was definitely not fun growing up without a lot of money. Phone service disconnections, car repossessions, and collection calls were common occurrences. The absolute worst experience was not being able to buy classmates birthday gifts. I remember looking around the house for the least used-looking thing to give. I tell you all of this to set the stage for my early interest in creating wealth.

I came across a copy of Napoleon Hill's *Think and Grow Rich* when I was twelve years old. Then I discovered Jack Canfield and Tony Robbins. Their stories of overcoming less than optimal circumstances resonated deeply with me. The central message of these books, *The Secret*, and scores of others is that we can have, be, and do anything and everything. The distilled formula is simple:

1. Get clear about what you want.
2. Believe that it is on its way to you.
3. Act as if it is on its way.

Sounds straightforward enough. Did it work for me? Not so much. I had no problem imagining what I wanted. Developing the belief, however, that things would change in my life was another story!

I have since used my law office as a laboratory of sorts. I started questioning my now more than 20,000 clients about their beliefs.

I have learned to ask them after our asset protection matters have been completed for fear that they will think I'm a fruitcake and not hire me. Twenty-plus years of questions later, I have more than a little empirical data about cultivating beliefs that we can have, be, and do amazing things in this world. Without belief in forward progress, I don't see how it is possible to live at our full potential.

My dentist has a poster in his office that reads: "What would you do if you believed you couldn't fail?"

There is no limit—right? On the other hand, without a firm belief that great things will happen, why on earth would I bother making an extra effort in pursuit of my dreams. I would be far more interested in relieving stress with some chardonnay, Doritos, and social media bingeing than in achieving goals. Or as Canfield would put it, choosing activities that are stress-relieving as opposed to goal-achieving.

The real question, for those of us who wish to change any area of our lives, is how do I change my beliefs about what is possible for me?

The first step in changing a belief is the desire to do so. Most of us are firmly and contentedly fixed on various beliefs. This is called confirmation bias. We accept news accounts that comport with our beliefs and reject opposing views as nonsense.

Those of us who have the desire to change a belief must first be convinced that the object of the new belief is within the realm of physical possibility. Sadly, I will likely not become a gymnast or ballerina. No number of positive affirmations will make it so.

With an objectively achievable goal in sight, it helps to have evidence in order to nurture the requisite belief. This can be a combination of reviewing past achievements, and seeking role models of possibility in the world. I love to study late bloomers.

Colonel Sanders was sixty-two and the recipient of thousands of rejections when he launched a worldwide empire. The eighty-three-year-old marathoner Helen Klein was an overweight smoker when she was "only" fifty-five.

These are people who recreated their realities. Most of us can't believe something without seeing evidence that it is possible. This is the first building block of belief.

I strongly recommend the book *Roctogenarians* by Mo Rocca. It is not possible to read this book and not have an increased belief in what we are capable of achieving.

When Juliette Gordon Low was born in 1860, her statistical life expectancy was forty-five years. Perhaps she was unaware of this. It did not stop her from founding the US Girl Scout organization in 1912, at the ripe old age of fifty-one! Her efforts have changed the lives of millions of girls around the world.

As a booster shot for my concept of what is possible, I regularly ask my ninety-plus-year-old clients about their lives. The top responses to my requests for advice are to keep learning, keep laughing, and keep moving. I also sometimes type "achievements after 90" into my search engine. This is how I learned about Harriet Thompson, who ran the San Diego marathon at the age of ninety-one! And she only took up running at the age of seventy-nine. I thought it was an added bonus to learn that she wasn't the oldest one to run it.

From Shoeshine Boy to Mogul

My client, John, sold his business five years ago, for $80 million. With some newfound time on his hands, he told me how he made his fortune. At nine years old, John was a shoeshine boy in New

York City. His meager earnings were dutifully turned over to his mother to help the struggling household. John told me that he made it a point to learn something from each of his customers. Most were happy to oblige the spunky and hard-working kid. A few went out of their way to praise John and told him that he would be a great success one day.

John's school attendance was sporadic. He never completed high school. At an age when his contemporaries were in college, John ran a newspaper kiosk. It was there that he saw an old shoeshine customer named Phillip. Phillip was a self-made real estate mogul. He asked John what his ultimate goal was.

John shared his dream of manufacturing the vitamins and nutritional supplements that he read about in bodybuilding magazines. Instead of dismissing the idea as silly, Phillip invited John to visit him at his office to tell him more. Because pharmaceuticals were far beyond Phillip's professional expertise, he invited an adviser to sit in on the meeting.

The professional response to John's business idea was mixed. It was the early 1970s, and yes, the timing was right to be in the vitamin and nutritional supplement space. The problem, however, was that hundreds of other companies were jumping in at the same time.

Assured that the underlying business concept was not out in left field, Phillip relied on his belief in John's work ethic, and promptly offered him $10,000 for 5 percent of the proposed company.

Thirty-five years and three patents later, John is currently interviewing captains for his yacht. He tells me that his own belief in his success was never in doubt. He credits his mother, uncle, and his shoeshine customers for incubating and nurturing his unshakable belief. John's belief was his capital. Properly invested, it produced a fortune.

I have a few clients who won various lotteries. One of these winners won twice! Not the talkative type, he wasn't terribly forthcoming in response to my many questions about the wins. He simply said that on both occasions that he bought the tickets, he *believed* that they were winners. He told me that checking the numbers felt like a formality.

Belief is quite possibly our most precious capital commodity. How, then, do we develop the belief that great things are possible for us?

I learned from John and countless other clients that external messaging shaped his belief in himself. As I look back on my own elementary school years, with nuns who were allowed to hit us with whatever objects were available while they called us stupid and lazy, I wonder if John wasn't better off shining the shoes of kind people.

We can nurture our wealth creation abilities by deleting and counteracting as many external belief-killing messages as possible. Psychologists say we become the average of the five people we spend the most time with. Should these be critical people who have no belief in forward progress?

Dr. Phil says that it takes a thousand "atta boys" to counteract one "you're a dumb ass." It stands to reason that we should strive to limit contact with those in our lives who want us to believe we are "dumb asses."

One of the many negative, belief-stealing people in my life was Suzanne. The wife of a friend of my husband's, I was in her presence a few times a year. She could have taught classes on being mean. Suzanne's favorite insults were those that did not seem to be insults to others.

"Ann, you look *so* tired! You must be working way too hard, you poor thing!"

I studiously limited my contact with her, with one exception. Shortly after my first appearance on Dr. Phil's TV show, Suzanne and I were at the same get-together. Everyone there was so excited and supportive of my "moment of fame." I remember thinking that Suzanne cannot possibly have anything mean to say about my TV appearance. After all, I did not totally bomb or faint or throw up on *Dr. Phil.*

Well, I was wrong. As I entered the orbit of her conversation, everyone else was high-fiving me. Suzanne, by contrast, feigned outrage at how little airtime I had been given. This was not even a thought in my head until that moment.

As Maya Angelou said, "When someone shows you who they are, believe them the first time."

Positive affirmations can go a long way to counterbalancing the negative external messaging of broken people. Remember the ratio though. It will take a thousand positive, belief-affirming words to counteract one interaction with the "Suzanne" in your life!

Vanquishing Your Internal Naysayer

Let's now turn to internal belief limitations. What do you think is the number-one impediment to believing in your future success? Twenty years ago, I set about asking this question of what would become more than 20,000 clients, including lottery winners who lost it all. Most people reported feeling deep down that they didn't believe they deserved the object of their dreams.

Some people in a new financial or professional position don't believe they belong there. This is called "imposter syndrome." It is here that I part company with others in the positive mindset community. I believe that there is often some rational basis for feeling like an imposter or that we don't deserve something. I have some experience with this feeling.

About a million years ago, I was elected to the New York State legislature in my twenties. I knew less than nothing. Did I feel like an imposter? Absolutely. Was I right to feel like an imposter? Ye-es! Because I knew less than nothing!

What should someone in this situation do to get over these feelings? Positive affirmations? Yoga? A walk by the ocean? A spa day? None of these action steps are likely to fill the crater-sized holes in my knowledge. The only way to cure imposter syndrome is to acquire the necessary knowledge or methods for competent performance and take some action.

KNOWLEDGE + ACTION = POWER

This is physics! Knowledge alone gives me nothing more than correct answers on *Jeopardy!* We can begin acquiring the necessary information and methods by studying others in the position.

I had a role model as a new legislator. She was charismatic and dressed to the nines. She exuded confidence. One day, I saw this veteran legislator standing in line at the capitol post office. Here was my chance to get mentored! This was right after a one-cent increase in stamp prices. Remember before the forever stamps, we had to buy supplemental stamps?

I actually overheard the assemblywoman ask the clerk how much twenty one-cent stamps would cost. The clerk told her twenty cents. She then proceeded to ask how much thirty stamps would cost. I decided to seek out another role model.

We can further hone our belief that we deserve more wealth and other good things by protecting whatever we happen to have right now.

In the words of parents everywhere, "You aren't getting another [Barbie doll] until you take better care of the ones you already have!"

Erecting prudent legal structures, as discussed in chapter 3, to protect whatever we happen to have right now provides some proof to our subconscious that we are responsible stewards and cultivates the belief that we are deserving of wealth.

Acting in alignment with the wealth we wish to have is the third element of the classic "Law of Attraction": act as if you already have the wealth you want by taking some of the legal steps to protect whatever you happen to have right now.

I can't make much progress accumulating wealth if there is a huge hole in the bottom of my piggy bank. We can also act as if we have the wealth we want by sharing some of what we happen to have right now (for more on this, see chapter 11).

TAKEAWAYS

- Belief that good things are on the way is the most valuable commodity we can have.
- Delete the naysayers in your life.
- Surround yourself with and emulate positive people who have achieved great things.

8

If You Are Not Growing It, You Are Blowing It

No amount of money is inexhaustible. A mindset fixated on growing assets is essential if we wish to retain what we have. There is no group that needs to focus more on this than lottery winners and inheritance recipients.

One of my favorite maxims, which made no sense to me when I first heard it, is that "Money alone does not solve money problems." Members of the typical household juggling credit card, student loan, and mortgage debt will probably disagree with this. Someone who is $40,000 in debt surely believes that a windfall of $40,000 is the answer to her money troubles. The reality is that this fix is likely to be short-lived.

A look at the cringeworthy lottery statistics indicates that something more than money is needed to put a person on solid financial footing. An estimated 70 percent of lottery winners lose or spend most of the prize within a few years. Some winners will actually end up with less than they had before buying the lucky ticket. How could someone possibly blow through hundreds of millions of dollars?

The sad lottery saga follows a common storyline. In forty states, lottery winners are not allowed to remain anonymous. The lottery programs want to put your smiling face on billboards and in commercials to encourage others to buy tickets. If you are in one of the ten states where you can remain anonymous but start buying expensive toys, then family, friends, former friends, and wannabe friends will know something is up and come out of the woodwork.

The winner is besieged with charitable requests. The initial euphoria triggers very generous impulses. Most winners start out with a true desire to share their good fortune with friends and loved ones. The problem is, quite simply, that it will never be enough. People will keep asking for money until the winner finally says no—in which case, the relationship may be ruined. If they don't say no, then people will keep asking for gifts, loans, and investment capital for their latest hair-brained schemes, until there is nothing left.

What went wrong here? Initially, the winner viewed the windfall as inexhaustible. Unfortunately, there is no such thing. If the winner's actions are limited to using, consuming, and irresponsibly giving away the money, then yes, it will all be lost. Without an active plan to grow it, even a large amount of money will move gradually but surely in the other direction.

Wealth is dynamic—it is constantly moving. It flows between people, businesses, companies, and countries. At the individual level, if it isn't growing, it is shrinking. Think of a shark that must constantly move forward or die. If someone is not actively engaged in growing wealth, then they are almost certainly in the process of losing it.

If I am an out-of-control financial train wreck before coming into some money, there is little chance that I will magically be able to responsibly handle a windfall. This is especially true for those of us with financially chaotic backgrounds.

Negative money stories are roadblocks on the path toward wealth. It is a challenge to erase long-running scripts of family members fighting over money and not being able to have and do things because of money. Or worse, not having money but choking ourselves with credit card debt to have and do all of the things anyway.

It is important to recognize negative feelings we may have toward money if we hope to reframe things moving forward. My financially chaotic childhood left me with some special money stories. Friends calling my house to get the message that "phone service has been temporarily disconnected" due to unpaid bills; being voted captain of the bowling team but unable to go because no one in the house had a dollar to give me for admission. These financial low points were punctuated with some windfalls. My late grandmother's slip-and-fall sideline resulted in a few. The windfalls, which also included an inheritance, were promptly and inexplicably squandered.

Don't Let Fear Win

It takes courage to break free of familiar patterns—even when they cause misery. Suze Orman's must-read book *The Courage to Be Rich* hits the nail on the head. Everyone says that they want to be rich, but it can be downright scary to make the necessary internal and external changes. Fear is a huge impediment to wealth building.

The biblical parable of the talents shows us the wealth inhibiting effects of fear. The story concerns a wealthy man preparing for a trip. Prior to his departure, he gave three employees varying amounts of money (talents). After many months away, he summoned the employees for an accounting. The first two employees doubled what they had been given through commercial endeavors. They were rewarded with more money and greater opportunities. The third employee was afraid of putting the boss's money at risk. He chose instead to bury the money, thereby ensuring that it wouldn't be lost or stolen. He explained this to his boss and returned the exact amount of money he had been entrusted with. The boss was furious with what he called laziness and wickedness and cast away the fearful person who did not use his efforts to grow the capital entrusted to him.

I don't believe that it is possible for a fearful person to grow wealth. Nor do I believe that it is possible to retain what we have if we are not actively engaged in growing it.

I have more than a few examples of dealing with fear in my life. Fourteen years in elected office provided me with countless examples of fear-inducing, spirit-crushing people and situations—yay!

When I first decided to run for public office, I had two major obstacles. I had no money, and I was deathly petrified of public speaking. I had a plan whereby I reasoned that I could run a campaign without ever having to give a speech before a crowd. I decided that I would simply go door-to-door for five months and personally meet with all of my prospective constituents! If I visited 100 homes per day, I could get to know everyone personally and would not have to make a speech. Genius!

About one month in, I was advised by all of the seasoned political folks that missing debates sponsored by the dozens of civic groups in the community was unheard of. Skipping the debates would be insulting to the organizers and fatal to my chances of winning.

Rather than speak in public, I decided to end my campaign and told my sister, Lorri. She was an idealistic college freshman at the time and was crestfallen by the news. She urged me to stay in. She pointed out that even though I had no realistic chance of winning, the race gave me a platform to talk to people about important issues.

I was really in a quandary now. There were two painful options: confronting my fear of speaking before a crowd, or disappointing my beautiful and idealistic 18-year-old sister, then an aspiring political science major. In the end, I didn't want her to think of me as a coward for the rest of our lives. She agreed to come with me to the first debate.

If you think that I am about to tell you that I ended up doing a great job and it went amazingly well, you would not be correct. The incumbent was given fifteen minutes to make a statement, and then five minutes to answer audience questions. I was to follow.

His name was Doug Prescott. He was a very popular assemblyman, in his sixteenth year in office, with game-show-host looks and charm. He was funny, articulate, and well-informed, and the crowd loved him. I was dying.

When it came time for his questions, an audience member raised his hand and instead made a statement: "Assemblyman Prescott, I just want to thank you for everything you've done for the community, these many years. I want you to know that you have my full support and that of my neighbors."

This prompted a standing ovation. I begged Lorri to let us just leave! I was in a lion's den.

She pulled a scrap of paper out of her bag and began furiously writing: "Machiavelli used to pray for hostile crowds because it was that much more of a feat when he turned them around." Oh brother! I would have to do this.

When it was my turn, I approached the lectern as if it were the guillotine. I focused my gaze on a pleasant-looking elderly woman in the rear and tentatively went through my legislative goals for the community.

The first audience question was, "Why should we vote for someone with no record of achievement compared to someone who has served us for 16 years?"

My response was unprepared but authentic.

"Every career in public service has a beginning. You are all here for the beginning of mine. I hope that you will one day be glad about that. Whether you vote for me or not and whether I win or not, I commit to dedicating my efforts . . ."

You get the point. I was moved to be authentic in the moment. Though Mr. Prescott's smooth performance ran circles around mine, I managed to get a smattering of applause. This felt like a triumph. Lorri and I celebrated with ice cream while sporting what we called our "large Marge" sweatpants in front of late-night TV.

My belief in myself changed that night, and my life hasn't been the same since. This is not to say that I no longer have to battle fear when facing a new situation.

Once I overcame my crippling fear of public speaking, I actually came to enjoy it. I now regularly give wealth, estate-planning, and asset protection seminars to just about any group that will have me! A two-hour drive to address eight elderly VFW members on the benefits of a trust? Count me in!

Here and there, some enthusiastic audience members began encouraging me to consider doing TV. Wow—imagine being on TV. Maybe I could do that . . . I saw attorneys in other areas of practice give expert commentary on TV shows. It was a lovely thought, but truth be told, I would have been quite happy for these thoughts to remain just that. Then my cellphone rang.

It was a producer for *Dr. Phil.* Could I be in Los Angeles the next day to offer legal advice to a family on the show? I thought my head would explode.

The producer cut me a wide berth by acknowledging the last-minute nature of the request. She assured me that they would keep me in mind for other opportunities if I couldn't make it.

In that moment, I had three simultaneous thoughts: 1. Be careful what you wish for! 2. They would never call again if I didn't go now, and 3. I did not want to live the rest of my life feeling like a coward for saying no!

And so it was that I made my way to Stage 29 of Paramount Studios the following day. As I was escorted up to the stage to join Dr. Phil and the couple in crisis, I had only two thoughts: Don't pass out, and don't throw up on Dr. Phil!!

Then I focused on his guests. In this moment everything changed, and I discovered one of the most important tools for moving beyond fear and fostering unshakable belief in one's abilities: Move from thinking about *performance* in a given situation, and instead focus on *serving* people who need some help.

It is not possible to feel fear in a given situation when we can shift all our focus to serving others. I may not always have a perfect solution for those I am trying to serve. However, if I am motivated by a desire to help, and I commit to being authentic, only good can result. This may be as simple as acknowledging that I, too, am struggling with the problem the person in front of me is dealing with. At the very least, they will hopefully feel better knowing they are not alone.

Happiness experts tell us that we are more fulfilled while working toward goals. My client, Len, sold his company for a boatload of money. He and his wife celebrated with a two-month-long vacation on a secluded island at a premier resort. Len told me that by the fourth day on the beach with a cocktail in hand, he longed to be back in the trenches of his business. For him, the joy and fun was in the creation of his business. Fortunately, he recognized this and has started a new company. His wife has taken to traveling with friends.

Acquiring a Wealth Mindset

There are an inexhaustible number of ways to grow wealth. I heartily recommend that people start their wealth-building journey by reading David Bach's classic, *The Automatic Millionaire.* This book is a great primer on reducing wasteful spending and channeling the saved money toward debt elimination and creating a balanced investment portfolio.

We can acquire more methods or "how-to" elements of building our net worth by learning about people who have done what we want to do. We can take classes on developing wealth-building skills. We can find mentors and model their actions. Learning effective methods, while not necessarily easy, is pretty straightforward. Chances are you are not the first one to have embarked upon the specific wealth-building road you have selected. Success does, in fact, leave clues. You only need learn and adopt the methods employed by others.

Starting from Zero

Isn't it premature to think about protecting wealth and growing wealth when I have *nothing* right now?

I believe that there is more than a fair chance of staying at zero if we don't take steps to actively grow our wealth. It is a mistake to wait until one has money before working aggressively to grow what we do have. We must start with the proposition that we all possess valuable assets. This may require a more expansive definition of assets than just the contents of a bank account. John's work ethic (see page 114) was worth $10,000 and ultimately grew to $80 million. Creativity is another valuable commodity.

Newton's Third Law of Motion states that for every action, there is an equal and opposite reaction. What you put out there comes back to you.

This concept also forms the basis of the Golden Rule: Treat others as we wish to be treated. Put it out there and it will come back to you.

This is physics. Not woo-woo stuff. I don't believe that sitting on a throw pillow, willing a fortune into existence is a foolproof plan. Physics, on the other hand, cannot fail.

When I talk to people about growing wealth, the most frequent question I get is some variation on the following: "How the *#@! can I grow wealth when I have nothing? Don't I need capital to invest?"

Yes, we do. Those of us without traditional assets, however, simply need to be more creative as we start our wealth-building journey.

You don't need money in order to add value to every situation you are in. By creatively and systematically adding value to every encounter, it won't be long before the value returns to you in a tangible form. Some concrete examples are in order:

A few years ago, there was a bag left in my mailbox with a note from a new neighborhood dry cleaner. If I wished to give them a try, I was to leave my dry cleaning in the bag by my front door. If I did not want to try them, I was to leave the empty bag for them to pick up. I was impressed by the effort that went into this overture. They immediately set themselves apart from a typical new business. I learned later that the owner had no money for advertising.

She did, however, have ingenuity and the stamina to cover all the homes in our neighborhood. I have been a happy customer for many years now.

During the COVID-19 pandemic, I left a pair of my husband's pajama bottoms in the dry-cleaning bag with a note asking for them to be taken up four inches. The hemmed bottoms were delivered back a few days later with two face masks made from the extra fabric.

This was such a thoughtful and clever thing to do. It did not cost them anything to do this, beyond a few extra moments at the sewing machine. The value added to their relationship with me is incalculable. There is hardly a person I know, who has not heard this story. I have taken to actively encouraging my neighbors to go there. If you live on the North Shore of Long Island, New York, I hope to see you sometime at Cove Cleaners!

Think leaving a laundry bag and making a few masks aren't exactly transformative business ideas? You are right. That's the point. Any one of us is capable of putting just a bit of thought into creating value for existing and potential contacts and clients.

Another example of a company who invests in its customers in an "above and beyond" kind of way is the pet supply company Chewy.

A client of mine lost her dog to cancer. She contacted Chewy and asked if she could return the unopened packages of dog food and supplies from the most recent delivery. They agreed to issue a refund, but instead of taking back the unused supplies suggested that they be donated to an animal shelter! This cost them very little but was such a creative and lovely gesture. I have been sharing this story with all pet parents that I know.

Not content to stop adding value after creating a new raving fan, Chewy also sent my friend a dozen roses with a sympathy card on the loss of her furry family member. OK, the flowers cost money, but I know that this addition of value to the customer relationship will result in a return to them worth many times the amount spent.

Harnessing Value from Your Imagination

Some of you may be familiar with the so-called paperclip game, made famous by Kyle MacDonald. The Canadian man managed, over the course of one year, to trade a red paperclip for items of successively greater value, culminating in a house.

His first trade netted him a fish-shaped pen. He then bartered the fish pen for a custom doorknob made by a potter in Seattle. He traded the doorknob for a camp stove, which was then traded for a generator. The generator was traded for a beer keg and illuminated Budweiser sign. His creative powers were on full display when he marketed the sign and keg as an "instant party kit," which he traded for a snowmobile.

He continued his creative bartering until he netted a farmhouse in the town of Kipling, Saskatchewan.

"There are people all over the world, saying that they have paperclips clipped to the top of their computer, or on their desk or on their shirt, and it proves that anything is possible," MacDonald said in his TED Talk.

Perhaps of greatest interest, to me, is his follow-up statement "that the quest was more exciting than reaching the goal." Sounds like Mr. MacDonald would be well-served to embark upon his next wealth-building project before financially ruinous boredom sets in.

It has been said that you can't get what you want if you don't ask for it. A related bit of wisdom that I've heard more times than I can count is that "it doesn't hurt to ask."

I disagree with this. With some exceptions, I think that decision-makers are more inclined to give you what you want, if you first add value to the situation or relationship. Why do charities spend tens of thousands of dollars to host balls to inspire would-be donors to contribute money to their cause? Wouldn't it be more expedient and economical for the charity to simply reach out directly to the prospective donors and ask for contributions?

If this worked, they would certainly go that route, thereby saving a lot of money. Instead, the most successful charities have learned that by creating a targeted value proposition, intended donors gladly make generous contributions. The charity curates a beautiful environment, honors an influencer, and invites well-heeled guests who wish to mingle and be photographed with the honoree. These photos, in turn, are displayed at the donors' places of business. The hoped-for outcome being to raise one's prestige in the eyes of clients, colleagues, and customers.

This is Newton's Third Law at work again. By creating and giving value, it must come back to you. The trick is to recognize what valuable commodities you already possess and then strategically deploy (invest) them.

For most of us, our most valuable commodity is our unblocked imagination and creativity.

Remember the "Stone Soup" parable? This has been attributed to many different sources. The story involves a poor, hungry traveler who goes door-to-door asking townspeople for food. Everyone asked promptly refused.

Discouraged, hungry, and now tired, the traveler took a nap under a tree. He awoke with his hand upon a stone and an idea in his head. He now went door-to-door inviting townspeople to join him for a soup dinner that he would make from his magic stone. He simply needed a large pot filled with water. Then, just some salt and pepper. Next, maybe some carrots. As the soup became real, excited townspeople gladly brought forth their own contributions to the remarkable creation.

Some point to the Stone Soup parable as an example of the power of sharing. I disagree with this. The townspeople didn't seem very willing to share when the hungry traveler simply asked them for food to eat.

It was only by using his creativity that he offered something of perceived value to others. He floated an admittedly silly but intriguing and then exciting proposition that gained momentum of its own, until the original thought became reality. The traveler enthusiastically shared an idea—a value proposition which came back to him in tangible form.

Again, there are countless methods of building wealth. The central formula, however, is unchangeable: one must invest capital resources in something that will grow in value.

As we've seen in this chapter, those resources are not always in the form of cash. We can develop and invest belief and creativity in ways that will produce wealth. Another non-cash asset that can be honed and deployed to produce cash is frugality.

Reckless spending will erode our bottom line by reducing cash that would otherwise be growing and working for us. It simultaneously erodes our belief that we deserve wealth. If I am spending like a drunken sailor, I am not acting in alignment with being a responsible steward of wealth.

Please Don't Try to "Fake It 'Til You Make It!"

I am aware of a school of thought that encourages people to engage in aggressive spending in order to project an image of the lifestyle to which they aspire. This is absurd. Taking on debt and engaging in profligate spending causes anxiety, stress, and pain. How do you feel when you have an inbox full of bills that you are unable to pay in full?

This is a surefire way to sap one of the confidence and creativity needed to actually advance in business.

Chances are you have access to potential capital that you only need to grab and put it to work! I have several clients who are New York City Department of Sanitation workers. Each has told me that they routinely retrieve discarded household items and sell them as a side hustle.

The wildly successful entrepreneur, philanthropist, and motivation coach Dean Graziosi is an example of someone who built a fortune from nothing by recognizing and deploying some non-traditional capital resources. As a teenager, while working on a landscaping crew clearing property, he bought his own chainsaw to cut firewood from the felled trees. Instead of going out for beers with his buddies after hours, he worked on his firewood business. It became so profitable that Graziosi was able to make a down payment on investment real estate.

Graziosi did not have a lot of early advantages. He was raised by a single dad who was so broke at times that they slept in a bathroom and had to bathe with cold water. In his book, *The Underdog Advantage,* he makes a compelling case that adversity nurtured a palpable desire, which he strategically honed to build an empire!

We all have unique access to resources that can be strategically deployed to create wealth. I have yet to meet the person who can't scour their homes for items to sell and generate some capital with which to pay down debt, invest, and share.

TAKEAWAYS

- What valuable resources do you currently possess, and how can you cultivate and strategically deploy them for material benefit?
- Become an agent of positive change for others. This is guaranteed by physics to produce positive change in your own life.

9
The Laws of Time and Money

When asked what the most precious commodity on earth is, what do you think a 98-year-old billionaire would reply? Time, of course. No discussion of growing wealth would be balanced without focusing on how we tend and cultivate or waste the valuable resource of time. Unlike money, we can't increase our available time. We most certainly can, however, learn how to make maximum productive use of time in order to achieve more wealth.

How we choose to invest the valuable resource of our time bears a direct relationship to the value that will redound to us in the form of tangible wealth. We are all allotted twenty-four hours per day. One-third of these hours are to be spent sleeping.

Evolving research indicates that how well we sleep has profound influence on how productive, happy, and healthy the remaining sixteen hours are.

Sleep is the period during which our bodies carry out vital repair and restoration tasks. Our immune systems fight and repel disease-causing pathogens; we neutralize age-accelerating free radicals and our conscious minds get a desperately needed break from the weight of daily stress.

After a good night's sleep, our bodies and minds are refreshed. We feel energized, optimistic, and ready to take on the world. Sleep deprivation, on the other hand, leaves us irritable, unproductive at work, more likely to have an accident, and more likely to become ill.

The Centers for Disease Control and Prevention reported in 2024 that lack of sleep had become a public health issue. Studies across the world tell us that we have never slept fewer hours, or less soundly. Survey respondents report record-high levels of individual stress, which keeps us awake at night. The resultant lack of sleep increases our levels of stress during the day.

A recent Bankrate.com survey revealed that more than 50 percent of Americans cite money stress as the top factor preventing them from falling asleep at night. A sleep-deprived employee or entrepreneur, in turn, will suffer financially. How can we break the grip of this vicious cycle?

We can start by prioritizing our sleep. Unplug, try not to think about your annoying coworkers, and keep a pad and pen nearby. Jot down next-day action items that come to mind, so you can quickly escort the thoughts out of your head without fear of forgetting them tomorrow.

Some people eschew the need for sleep. I've heard various hard-charging types say things like "sleep is for the weak," "work hard play hard," or my favorite, "there will be plenty of time for sleep when I'm dead." Sleep and death are connected, but probably not in the way that quote suggests. A study of the science of sleep indicates that failure to give our bodies enough of it may indeed hasten one's death. Conversely, adequate sound sleep, which gives our bodies a chance to recharge and repair, should enable our bodies to last longer.

The emerging field of chronobiology tells us that there are differences in sleep habits and needs between people. The composer Arturo Toscanini is said to have slept only five hours per day. President Calvin Coolidge, at the other extreme, slept eleven hours each night. Most of us fall somewhere in between.

The most cited of Benjamin Franklin's lifetime compendium of aphorisms and pithy advice is "Early to bed and early to rise makes a man healthy, wealthy, and wise."

This is a struggle for many. I am a big fan of the writer Robin Sharma and devoured his book, *The 5 AM Club.* He makes a compelling case for the wonders of being awake and working in the magical predawn hours of each day. He convinces us that by pushing through the discomfort of a predawn reveille and wrestling an extra hour of productive time out of each day, we will have thirty "extra" hours each month.

Scientific studies indicate that this is more of a struggle for some people. Jeremy Campbell's 1987 book *Winston Churchill's Afternoon Nap* introduced many of us to the concept of "larks." These are people who naturally produce epinephrin in the morning, thereby stimulating the flow of nutrients and oxygen in the body. I definitely skew more toward the morning person or lark model of sleeper.

Eager to claim my extra productive hours promised by *The 5 AM Club*, I gave it a shot. Though I don't manage it every day, on the days when I am able to do it, my ensuing day is definitely a step above average! I find that I am most easily able to get out of bed at this viscerally difficult hour when I promise myself a nap later in the day.

There is a strong case to be made for the beneficial effects of daytime naps. It is said that Winston Churchill routinely slept for about an hour each day after lunch—even during World War II. More recently, a study has found that people who nap regularly, even for twenty minutes, have lower risk of heart attack and stroke compared with non-nappers.

By prioritizing and making improvements to the amount and quality of our sleep, we will have more energy and optimism during our waking hours. Our efforts to grow wealth, in turn, will be more powerful and productive. Once properly rested, we can turn our attention to other opportunities to redeploy and direct our time in order to grow wealth.

Strategic Investments of Our Waking Hours

Who do you choose to spend your precious sixteen waking hours with? We all know that we should surround ourselves with the right people. We all have people in our lives that build us up and those that tear us down. Some of the latter are "energy vampires" (such as Suzanne, who I introduced you to in chapter 7), who appear to derive satisfaction from others' misery and misfortune. Their negative influence on others cannot be overstated. These are people to be avoided at all costs. Unfortunately, they are often professional colleagues.

The political arena exposed me to the best and the brightest as well as the washed-up and miserable. A clear member of the miserable camp was Lucy. She was the long-suffering wife of one of my philandering colleagues in the legislature. She truly seemed to delight in putting me down. I am definitely not an overly sensitive person. Fourteen years as an elected official, with countless doors slammed in my face, has left me with a good supply of emotional armor. Lucy, however, had a particular set of mean-girl skills.

One such encounter took place when I was eight months pregnant and feeling less than my best. Upon arriving at a party, she made a beeline for me, gave me a fake hug and air kiss, then actually said, "Poor thing—retaining water, right?"

I was momentarily speechless, but figured my only response was to let her think that I was unaware of my very bloated state. So, I replied, "Thankfully not yet . . ."

I could tell by her face that she desperately wanted to correct me, but she somehow held herself back. Truth be told, she was right. Not only was I eating dessert during pregnancy, I was eating it after lunch as well as dinner! Still—I was definitely sidetracked by Lucy's cruelty.

Should I have been able to totally disregard her thoughtless comment? Probably. The reality, though, is that I couldn't. I spent more time than I care to quantify thinking up better comebacks I could have lobbed. This negative encounter cost me precious time. Time that could have been spent on growing my then fledgling law practice.

I am sure that toxic people like these are struggling with their own demons and that I should have compassion for them. For me, however, this compassion is best felt from a distance. The lesson I took from my last encounter with Lucy is that I should go out of my way to avoid future encounters. If I ever see her again, I will keep moving as she gives me the fake air kiss!

It is said that we become the amalgam of the five people we spend the most time with. Napoleon Hill long encouraged his many readers to form what he referred to as a "Master Mind" group—a practice he learned from the wealth-growing master, Andrew Carnegie.

A few years back, I experimented with forming such a group. I called it "Money Magnets."

Once a week, we got together in my office conference room and shared ideas for saving money and growing wealth. We discussed weekly struggles and spending temptations and offered each other boundless positive feedback and encouragement. This weekly expenditure of one hour of time produced dividends in the form of a better financial bottom line for all participants.

When people with similar goals interact, some very creative problem solving can be unleashed. The aggregate total of valuable ideas unleashed by a group working in harmony is greater than the sum total of that produced individually by each member. Most of us are social creatures who thrive in the right group. Our different backgrounds and experiences push each other beyond our habitual ideas. Top businesses have long benefited by this principle when creating working groups to innovate and tackle problems.

Those without a ready bench of talented and positive team members with whom we can soar would do well (once again) to become creative.

A few years back, I attended a Tony Robbins live event called "Unleash the Power Within." I feel that it was definitely worth the investment of time and money. I would challenge anyone to attend this event and not walk away with fresh ways of looking at things and new ideas with which to better use time to achieve a more rewarding life.

Aside and apart from the incomparably dynamic Mr. Robbins and his ultra-high-energy team, the interaction between fellow attendees was transformative. It was moving to be surrounded by thousands of people from nearly every country in the world, from all walks of life, who made it to Los Angeles with shared goals of developing new perspectives and a desire to create more financially secure and otherwise fulfilling lives.

I am intrigued by people who are constantly striving for something better. We came together from varied economic, educational, religious, and cultural backgrounds, yet we were in many important respects fellow travelers.

Those who consistently use their free time to inform and improve themselves are the ones who achieve financial growth. It is easy to stay in our comfortable holding patterns. But will doing the same things, with the same folks, day after day, year after year, produce different results? Probably not. Spending a few days with the Tony Robbins folks from wildly different backgrounds had an energizing effect. Have you ever had dead flashlight batteries that worked again after you turned them upside down? Exposure to positive thought leaders can help us turn our timeworn and stultifying thinking patterns upside down.

Scheduling some virtual exposure to the top minds in personal finance and wealth achievement can help unleash a slew of fresh ideas. In response to the COVID-19 pandemic, many time-maximization leaders such as Tony Robbins and Jack Canfield developed virtual content and programs to replicate some of the transformative effects of their live events. Time spent absorbing energizing content may prove to be a better investment of time than playing spider solitaire.

The next arena where regular investments of time can produce huge financial dividends is fitness. Why on earth, you ask, am I going off on a fitness tangent in a book about growing wealth?

The answer is that I know from personal experience that my best business and wealth-growing ideas have come to me during or shortly after a jog or power walk. Stimulating blood flow brings more oxygen to the brain. Exercise releases nature's feel-good drug, endorphins. As if this were not enough, exercise reduces stress. This leaves me less focused on trifling annoyances, and better able to focus my time and thoughts toward more positive and productive ends.

This all sounds great, but why aren't most of us getting enough daily physical activity? After a mentally and physically draining day, we simply don't feel like it. This is Newton's First Law at work: ". . . a body at rest stays at rest." It is more than a little ironic that when we are feeling drained and demoralized, we have zero interest in doing the one thing nearly guaranteed to switch our mental states back to positive.

I don't claim that I am always able to wrestle my lazy self onto the treadmill. However, a technique that often works for me is to imagine that I am taking an "exercise vitamin." Doing jumping jacks or a plank as the water boils for my cup of tea is so much better than doing nothing. My five-or-ten-minute exercise vitamins are an example of not letting the perfect be the enemy of the good!

The world's most financially successful people regularly invest time in their physical fitness. Time spent optimizing physical conditioning is an investment in one's financial bottom line. Physical activities boost our moods, enable us to sleep better, and stave off illnesses. With less sick time, we can devote more time to wealth-building activities.

Study after study demonstrates that physical activity can actually add years to our lives. This is one of the smartest investments of time that we can possibly make. I *try* to spend as close to one hour a day as possible on physical fitness.

Those aspiring to incorporate more fitness into daily life might do well to avoid throwing away money with little prospect of significant fitness returns. It costs nothing to park farther away from the store to increase total daily steps. Joining a gym or purchasing a piece of exercise equipment from an infomercial, on the other hand, is more likely than not a waste of money. The overwhelming majority of folks who join gyms never set foot there. An unused gym membership is a negative double-whammy—not only are we taking money from our bottom line and transferring it to owner of the gym, we have added another item to our list of things that we know we should be doing but aren't.

Battling Our To-Do Lists to Free Up Time

Who doesn't have an endless list of things that need to be completed? A stack of bills to be dealt with, thank-you cards to be written, articles to be read? This ever-growing list is a negative element in our daily lives. The so-called Zeigarnik effect explains that our brains focus more on unfinished tasks, compared with tasks that we actually accomplish.

There must be some evolutionary underpinning to this. Perhaps our tribe was more likely to survive the winter if we fixated on the berries yet to be harvested as opposed to what we already collected and ate?

Psychologist Hadassah Lipszyc studied the effect of incomplete tasks on our sense of well-being. Her conclusion was that incomplete tasks and procrastination led to generalized anxiety and loss of our precious commodity of sleep.

My approach to dealing with the to-do list is to be extremely selective about what makes it there in the first place. We hate to say no to friends and acquaintances who ask us to do things and go places. Saying no on the front end, however, saves us from energy-zapping dread and malaise.

With respect to items already on the list, it is a good practice to proactively reduce the list. It is a liberating feeling to admit and then decide that not everything we initially thought we needed or wanted to do is the best use of our limited time. My husband is more rigid about leaving his to-do lists intact. His bedside table holds a mountain of magazine and newspaper articles.

I see this as a daily visual reminder to him that he isn't doing everything he thinks he needs to do. How can visual cues of being ineffective not reduce one's energy, optimism, and efficiency?

Optimizing Time Spent at Work

Without exception, whether employee, employer, independent contractor, sole proprietor, or entrepreneur, people report challenges dealing with work colleagues. Like it or not, most of us spend half of our waking hours with our coworkers. Unfortunately, these relationships can be a source of frustration and anxiety. Given the amount of time we spend at work, negativity here will not only harm our career prospects, it will cloud every other area of life. Stress from negative work interactions follows us home and robs us of time by interfering with our enjoyment of loved ones and leisure activities.

There is a simple test for assessing your feelings about your colleagues and work atmosphere. In the morning, as you approach the front door to your place of business, how does the pit of your stomach feel? Most people I ask report feeling slightly miserable. Nauseated is another common response. Why is this?

The short answer given, when I ask this question, is that their coworkers are quite simply a bunch of dysfunctional misfits. This may well be.

When we assemble any group of people, there is no escaping the statistical reality that most of them are struggling with their own demons. Out of any given ten adults, seven are sleep-deprived, four are divorced or considering divorce, two are struggling with dependence on a chemical substance, three are living with personality disorders, one is in an abusive relationship, and six simply report being unhappy. Go Team!

Is it any wonder that our attempts to approach a toxic and broken community with a cheery attitude are short-lived and do nothing to move the needle on the negative atmosphere ?

Earlier, I implored you to eliminate toxic people from your life. Unfortunately, this is not always possible in our work environment. As nice as it would be to press an eject button, and transport Harry in cubicle eight to outer space, we are stuck with him. Yes, it would be great if the company could fix things, but we shouldn't hold our breath. Low-grade misery at work can hobble our career and wealth-building prospects. The real question is: what we can do to turn things around?

Employers are gradually moving toward implementing programs to improve workplace morale. As in many other human resources areas, this trend is in response to legal liability. There is an emerging theory of legal liability for creating, fostering, or even merely allowing a hostile or toxic work environment.

As a result, you shouldn't be surprised to find an invitation to a team-building event from HR in your inbox. You may soon find yourself playing beach volleyball, zip-lining, or in a hot yoga class with your coworkers. In addition to your employer's efforts, there are some strategies you can adopt, immediately, to improve your work atmosphere right now.

Not your job? Well, it is your problem. Workplace stress has very real physical consequences. It can result in poor sleep and interfere with enjoyment of leisure time. Yes, it would be great if someone else would do something to turn things around. But, to the extent that stress over work seeps into other areas of our lives and can negatively affect our health, shouldn't we try to make things better?

It is a universal truth that we can't change other people. I recently read Mel Robbins's *The Let Them Theory.* The book very effectively drives home the point that we can't change people and that we are wasting precious time and mental bandwidth to even try!

We can, however, greatly improve the atmosphere in which we find ourselves. We can singlehandedly improve the atmosphere for everyone by adding value to work relationships.

I encourage everyone to try the following workplace challenge for thirty days. You can do this alone, or together with a colleague who also wants to be part of the solution. The points that follow are rooted in common sense. We knew these things in kindergarten. Taken together, and put into practice, the results have been transformative for everyone who has tried it.

Thirty-Day Workplace Challenge

1. **Treat your coworkers with true kindness because you are connected!** Maya Angelou wisely counseled that people will soon forget what you say, but they will remember how you made them feel. Make eye contact and share a warm smile. Why should you do this? There are reasons beyond it simply being the right thing to do. As much as we may wish to keep our distance from work colleagues, we are truly all connected. Miserable Martin in the next cubicle brings the overall atmosphere down. If there is anything at all that we can do to bring him up a bit, our own environment is thereby elevated. It doesn't make any sense to do anything to put Martin in a bad mood. Why would we want to bring down an element in our own environment?

   Yesterday, I was in a cranky mood. This was probably a result of lack of sleep. Practically everything and everyone—including my dogs—annoyed me. It would have been nice to take a mental health day, but I had some deadlines to meet, so into the office I trudged. I tried to view the mood as a bit of bad weather. Even though I was unable to make it disappear, it would soon pass. However, while it was with me, I made a conscious effort not to share it! I kept phone calls to a bare minimum and avoided interactions with my coworkers. I treated my lousy mood as contagious negative energy that I didn't want jumping onto my office colleagues.

2. **Take an interest in colleagues' outside pursuits.** I know that you may well prefer to be at the dentist than to learn about Comic Con. View it as an opportunity to increase your brain plasticity. If Jim's morale is better for having someone listen, you have singlehandedly improved the atmosphere for everyone. In the workplace, as in every other area of life, people don't care what we know until they know that we care! By allowing Jim to teach you something, you have empowered him. This is the action of a leader.
3. **Discard the competition mindset.** We are each running our own race at work and in life. The only useful comparisons are to ourselves. Yes, it stings that the boss promoted his unqualified nephew to the position that you deserved. Take the long view that this is merely an annoying speedbump. I know from experience that it is very easy to become fixated on things that seem unfair. Thoughts of unfairness or being cheated out of something you deserve is rooted in a belief that the supply of good things is limited. Stay focused on the thought that your continued efforts will result in something bigger and better for you. By looking beyond nuisance distractions and focusing on honing your talents and keeping your mind's eye on where you are going, you can't fail!

4. **The good things you seek are not in limited supply.** This one is foundational to the competition mindset. Only if there is a limited supply of good things do I need to take a sharp elbow to my colleagues. For thirty days (to start), I encourage you to think bigger. Well, you may be thinking, I work in an independent retail store and there can be only one opening for store manager. How am I supposed to work hard and aspire to this one position without showing the owner that I can do a better job than Carol?

   This question demonstrates the widespread but mistaken belief that the supply of good things is limited. I urge you to think bigger. Think bigger than the one store manager position that you can see in front of you. For thirty days, imagine that your entire team is working in harmony to see how profitable the business can become without keeping score as to who did what. With all of your sails pointed in the same direction for thirty days, you and Carol are no longer pitted against each other in your mind.

   One immediate result of this is that she won't annoy you quite so much. If you choose to keep this thirty-day experiment to yourself, Carol's behavior won't immediately change. However, you will be less annoyed by her because you are no longer in head-to-head competition. This, in turn, will free up your mental bandwidth.

   When we move beyond (even for thirty days) nursing perceived slights by coworkers, we immediately elevate our thoughts to those of creativity and growth. By generously pouring your efforts, creativity, and positivity into the business, you are doing a few things that benefit *everyone* involved. You are, for starters, elevating the overall mood in the workplace. This is an immediate benefit to every colleague and customer you interact with.

Discarding the scarcity and competition mindsets will result in the disintegration of perceived limitations and roadblocks. You will feel and actually be more positive. It is impossible for colleagues and clients not to notice this. People will want to join your island of positivity. When we stop competing with our colleagues for credit, we can share ideas for the growth of the business. We become a master-mind group in the spirit of the great Andrew Carnegie. When the company reaches the next level, so will you. Who cares if Carol becomes the store manager? When three more locations are opened, you can become the regional manager!

Time for Fun and Recreation

All work and no play makes Jack a dull and ineffective grower of wealth. The world's most successful people carve out time to pursue and develop passions. The Four-Hour series author Tim Ferriss shared stories of taking tango lessons in Argentina. I have a client who put life on pause to take a six-week cooking class in Paris. We can redeploy money and time formerly lost to lifestyle inefficiencies on curating a life of wonder and adventure. A life that serves to inspire our loved ones.

One of the first and best productivity books I read is *The 7 Habits of Highly Effective People*. My biggest takeaway from this book is Stephen Covey's emphasis on what he called "Quadrant Two" activities. The specific activities will vary between people but are those that serve to energize and invigorate. Ballroom dance, water skiing, or attending a play or a concert are all possibilities. Rather than feel guilty about time not working, Mr. Covey urges us to wrestle these blocks of time from an otherwise unpunctuated conveyor belt of tasks.

Some workaholics eschew the importance of scheduling recharging time into the week. Mr. Covey shared a vignette about a man up in a tree, sawing a branch with a dull saw. His neighbor yells up to him, asking if he wants to sharpen the saw. The man in the tree can't hear him but shouts back that he is busy sawing the tree and will talk to him later. How much more efficiently can we achieve goals if we invest time "sharpening our saws" by having some fun and learning new skills?

Ideally, we are paying for our "Quadrant Two" adventures and activities with interest income generated by our wealth-growing activities. If we find the right wealth-building vehicles, we can, to a great extent, step back and allow time to transform even modest amounts invested into substantial assets. When asked about his greatest discovery, Einstein famously answered "compound interest."

Buying Time

Most people who know me would probably call me a cheapskate. I don't disagree with this. I am very deliberate about what I buy and force myself to forego discretionary purchases as long as possible. There are some expenditures, however, that can free up so much time that they pay for themselves many times over.

Rory Vaden gave an amazing TED Talk called "How To Multiply Your Time." One of the main takeaways for me was the wisdom of investing time into creating processes and systems to automate time-consuming tasks. Setting up automatic bill paying is a great example of "buying time." Gadgets that free up precious time include robotic vacuums, clear food storage containers, automatic pet feeders, and self-driving lawnmowers.

TAKEAWAYS

- How we choose to invest the valuable resource of our time bears a direct relationship to the value that will redound to us in the form of tangible wealth.
- Prioritize and optimize sleep.
- Don't waste precious time with negative energy vampires.

10
Becoming a Money Magnet

If you are currently in debt, I can relate! Upon graduation from law school, I had amassed more than $100,000 in student loans and more than $20,000 in credit card debt. At the time, my credit card company had a rewards program based on points earned by cardholders. The points were a function of your unpaid balance each month. Able to swing only the tiny minimum payments each month, I was doing pretty well in the eight-month-long reward program! At the end of eight months, my reward points entitled me to select from "prize" options. I was the proud new owner of a pair of candle holders. Vaguely aware that I'd been had, I didn't really dig deeply into the specifics.

From the clear light of my now militantly debt-free life, I shudder at the numbers involved. With $20,000 in revolving debt, at a 19 percent annual interest rate, I was racking up about $316 in interest each month. Note that current credit card interest rates can exceed 30 percent! I don't recall the exact amount of the minimum monthly payments, but I know that they were less than $100. My total debt was actually increasing each month—even without my regular pilgrimages to Bloomingdale's. Over the course of the eight-month reward promotion, I accrued more than $2,500 in interest. My reward for this was a pair of candle holders that probably could have been purchased from a dollar store. I still have the candle holders and think of them as my stupid trophy.

What on earth was I thinking? The answer, of course, is that I was not thinking. In my mind, there was little difference between money and credit. They each represented purchasing power. Every once in a while, one of my many credit cards would inexplicably raise my credit limit. I can remember lying awake at night planning my next purchases for the following day.

I was on an express train to a lifetime of dread and misery. I was not alone on this train (though I may have been the best dressed thanks to my shopping habit). The average American has more than $7,000 in credit card debt. Our outstanding national student loan debt has exceeded $1 trillion. Add to this mortgages and auto loans, and it is fairly common to have combined debt equal to or greater than our annual household income. Consider the following very typical illustration:

Jim is unmarried and earns $75,000 as an insurance claims adjuster. His monthly take-home pay after withholdings is $3,750. The outstanding mortgage on his home is $100,000. He has credit card debt of $12,000, a car loan of $13,000, and outstanding student loan debt of $32,000. Jim's annual combined interest payments on his loans are $7,710. Even if we subtract the portion of his mortgage payment going toward principal, and is therefore, not lost as an asset, the picture is not pretty.

Jim is working two months each year just to earn the interest needed to simply stay current with his loan payments. Over the course of a 40-year career, he will have spent more than 6½ years creating wealth—*for his lenders*!

Jim's story is very sad and also very common. Debt is truly an evil monster. It robs us of our wealth, our precious time, and our joy. How on earth do we allow this to happen? I was not a dumb person. The countless Jims out there are not necessarily dumb. When young adults are asked about their goals and dreams, how many will choose working 6½ years to benefit rich strangers that they will never meet? The concept is downright absurd.

The flip, but accurate, answer to the question of how we allow this to happen, is "very easily." When it comes to debt, as with so many other areas of our lives, we replicate the behavior of the people we spend the most time with. Parents, brothers, sisters, cousins, friends, and neighbors are statistically almost all in debt. Sadly, this condition doesn't seem to slow down their acquisition of yet more consumer goods!

We make self-conscious, weak, joking references to our collective condition. The term "retail therapy," for example, lets us know that we are not alone in our sorry state. It is clear, or at least should be, that we must summon the courage to break free from the death grip of consumer debt.

The odds of breaking free are unfortunately stacked against us. Lenders don't operate in a vacuum. They have very powerful help in the form of our elected officials and Madison Avenue.

Acting Rich Can Prevent You from Becoming Rich

Banks and other lenders are among the most powerful political lobbying forces in the nation. They pour untold millions into the campaigns of candidates for office on the state and federal levels, on both sides of the aisle, who show promise as "debt enablers." Like a wolf guarding the chicken coop, banks routinely have significant say in consumer protection legislation, such as the US bankruptcy code.

Why, for example, can student loan debt generally not be discharged in a bankruptcy proceeding? Without delving into the theoretical pros and cons for this rule, the sobering reason for its existence is that the lenders successfully lobbied against student loan discharge. Did the consumer protection advocates have a chance? Apparently not.

The most effective of the forces that keeps us lined up like morons at the trough of credit, with which to buy more stupid stuff that we don't need, is the advertising industry. Social media, TV, and movies are perfectly positioned to drive home the message that we need a never-ending array of consumer goods in order to be happy. Ads and social media successfully convince us that our stress and malaise (caused, in large part, by our financial turmoil) can be cured by even more stuff. Diabolically brilliant, Batman!

Never before have we been more connected to celebrities and social media personalities. The time spent with these folks has elevated them to the status of those people who we spend the most time with. We are, accordingly, very susceptible to their influence.

It has been said (by people who are a lot smarter than I am) that we are poised at the precipice of the information economy. When, in the history of mankind, have we ever had access to more thoughts, ideas, and information? Today's youngsters no longer have to be bothered with the quaint and tedious practice of reading books. Everything that they need or want to know seems to be contained in their phones.

Through YouTube, TikTok, and podcasts, they ardently and constantly follow social media stars. There is nothing new about adolescents worshiping idols. However, unlike the musicians, actors, and sports figures of yore, today's adolescent heroes all seem to be hawking goods. News accounts of barely post-adolescent billionaires should elicit more than a bemused eyeroll. We have all witnessed the inexplicable winds of chance and fortune that turn folks with little talent into mega-celebrity actors and recording artists.

This is different. Not only do our kids want to buy the stuff being pushed by social media personalities, but many of them think that they, too, can become top-level influencers. They just need to buy a bunch of junk, such as frisbees or friendship bracelets, in order to get a brand ambassador deal with a manufacturer. Our adolescent pack animals then support each other by buying one another's junk.

Admittedly, there is nothing new about targeting young people for financial gain. I can remember thinking I'd get rich selling greeting cards. I just had to buy the supply up front. Then I thought I was a world class artist because I nailed my art school entry. My replica of the pirate sketch on the matchbook must have been pretty darn amazing.

Fortunately, I did not have access to the needed tuition money. I did, however, scrape together the funds for the X-ray glasses to see through people's clothes. Even though they didn't work, I went to confession for even attempting to see through the nun's habits in elementary school.

This was an early lesson (lost on me at the time) in wasted money, with my X-ray glasses causing me to also waste time in the form of having to go to confession.

In recent years, however, our youth is increasingly targeted to buy a lot more stuff. Add to this the plentiful supply of credit being pushed on them at earlier ages, and we have a dangerous combination.

Avoid the Shackles of Credit

I qualified for my first credit card as a college freshman at the age of eighteen. In retrospect, this was a recipe for disaster. For the first time in my life, I could have and do everything I wanted. The local shopping mall was my new pleasure palace. It was like a sugar high. When the first bills came in, I realized that I had no money to pay them.

I then went back to the shopping mall. This time for a job. I was now a newly minted sales associate at the Gap. Thanks to the company's very generous employee discount, together with a Gap credit card, I quickly became one of their best customers! The only problem now was that I had to walk nearly a mile to catch the bus to get to my job. If only I had a car . . .

My next stop was a Nissan dealership! Through a combination of lax underwriting, an eager car salesman, and my own bad luck, I qualified for a lease on a brand-new red Nissan Sentra. Wow! The next problem was that I now needed to work full time at the Gap to afford the car payments, insurance, and, of course, all of my new Gap clothes.

This left little time for classes. I was now working full-time at the mall in order to pay for a bunch of stuff that I didn't need instead of filling my mind with the education that my student loans were paying for at the nearby college campus. My grades were abysmal. I did, however, learn world-class sweater folding skills!

I was a complete train wreck with no concept of financial security. Again, my only use for money and credit was to buy things. I remember being out with girlfriends around this time. The conversation turned to a mutual acquaintance, who was said to have $10,000 in the bank. I remember thinking that this was insane. Imagine all of the things she could be buying! Why on earth would someone let money go to waste in a bank like that?

How could a reasonably intelligent person be so utterly stupid? It is pretty simple. No one in my life or on television seemed to prioritize saving money and growing financial security for its own sake.

The people I saw on *Dynasty* were lucky to have so much stuff. The people on *Little House on the Prairie* (my favorite show of all time) would probably also have had lots of great things if only Oleson's Mercantile extended more credit!

Fast forward to the present—one of my core principles is to take 100 percent responsibility for everything that happens. This being said, it is not my intention to cast blame on anyone around me growing up. Any childhood financial anecdotes that I share are intended to help others recognize their own situations and consider following my exit route out of the morass. I also offer some glimpses into my family's financial mess to add some context to our national consumer debt statistics. Having worked with more than 20,000 families as an estate-planning attorney, I have come to learn that my stories are not that unusual.

As a child, I was aware of household bankruptcies and where we were at any given time. I knew that when enough time went by, we could get credit cards again. Not once do I recall hearing anyone speak of saving money.

I remember my mother coming into some money upon the death of her grandmother. To be fair, I do not know how much it was, or how long it should have lasted. I do remember frenzied shopping and then having no money again.

Car repossessions were not uncommon, nor were foreclosures. In retrospect, the last one should have been predicted and avoided. Somehow, there was enough money for a 10 percent down payment on a modest home. However, the household income was insufficient to qualify for a mortgage. Undeterred, my mother found a CPA to create copies of bogus tax returns showing artificially high income. We actually celebrated being approved for the mortgage. The inevitable foreclosure was delayed by my mother's plan to rent out a room in this very small house. The tenant was a former high school classmate. The situation was beyond embarrassing.

Any household in debt has their own similar stories. The stress, fear, and embarrassment caused by being in debt afflicts most of our nation's households in one form or another. The 50 percent of Americans who report difficulty sleeping cite stress over money as the top reason.

To soothe jangled nerves caused by financial difficulties, many turn to temporary fixes in the form of alcohol and drugs. Added to these horrors is the effect of financial despair on our relationships with loved ones. Money problems are the number-one cause of divorce and other breakups. This statistic has been borne out in my work with thousands of families. The divorce further tightens the financial vice because couples now have to split meager (if any) assets, for each party to establish their own household. That is, what's left after the many thousands paid to the divorce attorneys.

Stop the Out-Of-Control Financial Train

For me, the first step out of my financial swamp was developing an awareness of how bleak the situation was coupled with a desire to turn things around. Being turned down for a BMW lease was a blessing in disguise. I never wanted to be in that situation again, and I made a commitment to get out of debt and start saving some money.

I advise people at this stage to surround themselves with other people who prioritize saving. At the time, I did not know any such people. Instead, I got a library card and devoured books on money and finance.

I imagined that the authors were speaking directly to me. I was cultivating a group of imaginary friends.

My new friends included a group of women called the Beardstown Ladies. They were a group of mature women who formed a small but successful investment club, then authored a book of advice, *The Beardstown Ladies' Common-Sense Investment Guide*. They shared their tips for frugal living for the purpose of investing and growing the money not otherwise wasted.

I also got a lot out of the Heloise series of books from the 1950s. Many of these tips have little direct applicability to today's households. But while there is little chance I will ever apply the money-saving tips I gleaned for laundering crinoline skirts, it was instructive to be exposed to these ideas nevertheless. Reading about genius hacks for repairing, repurposing, and giving new life to things we already have helped me to reprogram my spending. Rearranging things to produce a new result is a metaphor I come back to often.

One of my favorite scenes in the sci-fi movie *Limitless* is when Bradley Cooper's character, with the aid of a mystery pill designed to enhance brain functioning, sets about transforming his surroundings. He rid himself of junk, rearranged his furniture, and rolled up his sleeves and cleaned. Without adding or buying as much as a matchstick, he was now living in a totally different environment.

We can and should be curating our surroundings to create a tranquil, organized, and calming influence. Doing this without spending money is a great activity to complement our early debt-elimination efforts. Throw out what's shot. Give away items that could still have use to someone else. Repair, repurpose, and organize what's left.

I have always functioned better in organized surroundings. I was an eager reader of Marie Kondo's *The Life-Changing Magic of Tidying Up*. I probably took her teachings to an extreme, parting with one or two things that I now regret. However, given that eight large garbage bags were purged from my already pretty orderly home, I estimate that 99 percent of what I parted with was spot on.

What I really appreciated about the author's early advice was that fancy storage containers and bins were not necessary for optimal organization. The storage container industry is a source of major annoyance to me. Not content to have foisted upon an unsuspecting public truckloads of junk that we don't need, they now want to sell us a bunch of pretty bins within which to store our stupid junk. When I heard that Marie Kondo now has a branding deal with a storage bin manufacturer, I wondered if future printings of the book will edit out her opposition to buying what she originally called "unneeded containers." Just saying . . .

A Penny Saved Is a Penny Earned

I vowed to eliminate nearly all discretionary spending, and at the age of 30, I opened my first savings account. It is still sort of unbelievable to me that I was a practicing attorney and a duly elected New York State assemblywoman without as much as ten dollars put away. My weekly stays in Albany still ended with me holding my breath as the hotel clerk swiped my credit card. But I was done with my old ways!

Saving money requires skill, discipline, and effort. For those, like me, for whom saving does not come naturally, self-study is in order. The mindset change from acquiring stuff to acquiring knowledge is a powerful force.

I endeavored to spend as much time as possible reading books about personal finance. Authors like David Bach, Suze Orman, Dave Ramsey, and Robert Kiyosaki shared straightforward information about growing wealth. Their lessons resonated with me because I was ready to listen.

Some debt elimination experts advocate focusing first on paying down debts with the highest interest rates. Others recommend targeting the debts with the lowest outstanding balances. This was my method of attack. With every spare dollar, I would allocate one-half to savings and one-half to paying down my smallest debts.

Many debt experts advise us to focus first on establishing an emergency fund. Others advise keeping a single credit card available for emergencies and plowing every spare dollar into paying down debt. For me, I recognized that seeing even a tiny balance start to grow in a savings account would be a psychological boost. My two-basket approach to savings and debt reduction was right for me.

The act of saving money is a skill and also a metaphor for many areas of life. When I save a dollar, or resist the impulse to eat a donut, I am saying no to my inner child that wants to buy or eat something now! In the category of "better late than never," I was on my way to mastering the art of delayed gratification.

Without the ability to say no to ourselves and others, we don't have a chance of retaining and building wealth. Without this foundation, our lottery winners and other windfall recipients promptly blow it all. Some lucky people seem to be born with the ability to say no to themselves. Remember the famous "marshmallow experiment"?

Researchers in the early 1970s assembled a group of young children. Prior to exiting the room, a researcher placed a single marshmallow in front of the child and gave them permission to eat it. However, if they did not eat the marshmallow, they would be given an additional marshmallow as a reward when the researchers returned.

Through one-way mirrors in an adjoining room, the researchers studied and filmed the children. Some ate their marshmallow immediately. Some stared at them for a few minutes and then ate them. A handful of children managed not to eat them. The children who resisted the treats kept their gazes on points in the room other than the table before them. This was the seminal study on delayed gratification.

People who know me are surely sick of hearing about the "marshmallow experiment." For me, it is a metaphor for being able to control ourselves. In terms of being able to control what goes into my mouth, what comes out of my mouth, what comes out of my wallet, and what goes into my bank account, we are all works in progress.

My work as an estate-planning attorney has given me unique access to the financial details of my clients' lives. The thousands of families I have worked with represent nearly every age, profession, religion, education level, and background. From each client, I have tried to learn something. In response to my many questions about childhood circumstances, spending and savings habits, and career trajectories, I have gathered a lot of empirical data.

What You Earn Is Less Important than What You Save

One of the most surprising but inescapable takeaways from the numbers is the loose relationship between household income and net worth. My highest-earning clients do not, for the most part, have the highest levels of accumulated wealth.

My client Paul is a perfect illustration of why this is. Paul is a primary care physician who was an early investor and principal of a chain or walk in urgent-care medical offices in New York. They are making profits, hand over fist, and have been doing so for the past five years. Paul's annual gross income is approximately one million dollars. He and his wife, Margo, live in a gorgeous home, belong to a country club, have children in private school, take extravagant vacations, and, of course, have designer clothes by the boatload.

No, I am not about to tell you that they have a negative net worth. They do, however, have a shockingly low net worth. Paul works, on average, ten hours each day. This couple does not prioritize saving money. They don't feel the need to do so, given Paul's massive earning power.

The only reason that this family has a positive net worth is because of the life insurance policy all partners of Paul's company are required to carry. Paul's life insurance death benefit is roughly equal to two years' worth of his earnings. The named beneficiaries are his business partners, who are obligated by virtue of a so-called buy-sell agreement to use the death benefit to buy Paul's share of the business from his estate upon his death.

Given the fact that Paul and his family are managing to spend every cent he earns, the life insurance buyout would allow Margo and the kids to continue in their current lifestyle for only two years upon Paul's death. Their kids are in their early teens. They seem only mildly concerned when I point this out.

This family appears on the surface, to be living the dream. In reality, they are barely afloat, with no real financial goals in place.

I also serve as the attorney for Paul's parents, Millie and Eddie. Paul could learn a lot from them in terms of finances. Millie is a retired teacher and Eddie is a retired cop. They have a net worth approaching $2 million. They achieved this impressive financial feat without ever having earned more than $100,000 in a given year. How can this be? Their son earns ten times as much per year, yet has a lower net worth!

Millie and Eddie benefited from a unique financial education as children. They grew up during the Great Depression. Their respective families had no choice but to become masterful with saving and making do with less, or more often than not, with nothing. Far from romanticizing their impoverished childhoods, Millie and Eddie were determined to make life easier for their own children.

They probably made things too easy. I believe that Paul would have been much better off if he heard the word "no" once in a while as a child. His parents wanted to shield Paul from the deprivations of their own youth. By doing so, however, they failed to share their valuable wealth-building skills. Millie and Eddie can afford to have and do just about anything they want. Fortunately for them, they don't have a compulsion to have and do everything all at once.

No amount of money or income is limitless. Wild and undisciplined spending can lead only to financial pain. Paul is in his early fifties. He can still manage the ten-hour workdays. I am in the process of begging him to reevaluate his lifestyle. By reducing their material consumption, Paul and his family could easily save a quarter of a million dollars per year. By doing so, Paul could have $2 million set aside in eight years.

With even conservative investments, the passive income thereby generated could enable Paul to retire from practice. He would then have the option of selling his interest in the business to his partners and further boost his nest egg. If Paul follows this route, he will have traded the appearance of prosperity for actual wealth. He will also have freed up days, months, and years to spend with his family.

From Public Assistance to the One Percent

My escape from financial pain began with the determination to stop buying dumb stuff and instead, invest available resources into assets that increase in value over time.

What are the best wealth producing assets? There are an unlimited number of asset classes capable of growing in value. From my 20,000+ clients, I've gleaned more than a few tips about amassing wealth. My advice to people starting out on this journey is to not get out too far over your skis. The best investment to start with is something that you know about already or can quickly learn.

As I made the decision to crawl out of my credit card coma, I read a lot of books on wealth building. The ones that resonated most with me were from Robert Kiyosaki's Rich Dad Poor Dad series. These books, of course, led me to real estate!

After being turned down for the BMW lease, I was determined to finally get my financial act together, so I spent the next few years dramatically reducing my spending. I paid off my credit cards and saved up $50,000, with which I planned to buy a used BMW.

Budding financial maven that I was, I reasoned that a gently used car would save me from the precipitous drop in value that occurs upon driving a brand-new vehicle off the lot. As the time to execute my well-deserved purchase drew near, I looked at the transaction with fresh eyes. Was this really the best and most productive use of $50,000?

The answer, of course, was no. With the exception of certain collectibles, most cars lose value every year. I ended up buying a used Jeep for $15,000 instead.

I took the remaining $35,000 and used it as a down payment on a four-family residential rental property in Albany, New York. The monthly rent income, less the mortgage payment, taxes, insurance, and utilities, generated a net profit of $900. This is the holy grail of positive cash flow, and I was hooked. The annual profit of $10,800 ($900 x 12 months) represented a near-30 percent annual return on my $35,000 investment.

Real Estate Investing 101

A glance at available listings in your neighborhood may not identify properties capable of generating positive cash flow. For this, it may be necessary to venture beyond your immediate vicinity. I would not, however, recommend going farther than a three-hour drive for the first investments. It is important to be able to get there easily when something comes up.

Though beyond the scope of this quick investment real estate introduction, there can also be significant income tax benefits. The specifics depend upon the laws in effect in a given year. We can usually deduct mortgage interest, property taxes, insurance, utilities, etc. from our income. We can usually also depreciate the property, which provides a "paper" loss and allows us to whittle down the total amount of income that is taxed. On top of these benefits is the internal appreciation in value enjoyed by most real estate in most markets over time.

Are there annoying phone calls about exploding toilets and water leaks? Absolutely. There are also deadbeat tenants who don't pay rent and other tenants who fight with each other. I had one tenant who drank too much and repeatedly passed out in the bathtub. He somehow never drowned but did manage to flood the downstairs tenants on a regular basis. He was a sweet guy and seemed genuinely sorry whenever I called him the following day. But clearly, investing in residential rentals is not a wealth-building activity that is right for everyone.

We can outsource many of the real estate headaches if we are willing to part with a small percentage of the profits. On some of my multifamily investment properties, I rely on a manager, whose job it is to screen prospective tenants and check credit scores and references as well as to collect rents and coordinate estimates for needed repairs. Is this worth paying 9 percent of the monthly gross rents? For me the answer is yes. This is another example of not letting the perfect get in the way of the good.

Before embarking upon any active wealth-building activity—to be distinguished from passively investing in mutual funds, for example—I encourage folks to consider the worst-case scenarios. In the investment real estate arena, these scenarios involve the inevitable expensive repairs.

I lose my mind when I see hucksters sell "no money down" real estate programs! Even if you are able to convince the seller to hold a mortgage, with the plan that the rental income alone will cover carrying expenses and allow you to pay the seller monthly, what is the plan when the roof needs to be repaired—or replaced!? Without some savings set aside as a cushion, a no-money-down real estate venture is an express train to financial ruin.

In addition to seriously considering what can go wrong, we would also do well to frankly assess our own skill sets. There are tons of wealth-building activities that I should steer clear of because I have zero talent in them.

In terms of real estate, I have never even contemplated getting involved with a "buy, fix, and flip" transaction. Like many people, I am an avid fan of house-flipping shows. These incredibly talented people seem to perform magic when transforming decrepit and dilapidated structures into elegant showplaces. They make it look easy. I cringe, though, at the prospect of people thinking they, too, can effortlessly accomplish such feats. I have seen enthusiastic investors borrow money from banks, friends, and family, with a surefire plan to make a mint with a house flip.

I can just about manage to hammer a nail into the wall. This enables me to hang pictures. My inability to even find the stud into which I should be hammering means that I am limited to hanging pictures that are lightweight. Given my inability to engage in any of the construction needed for a flip, I would have to pay retail for the work, thus making the process so costly as to not be worth it.

Though I steer clear of flipping, I do enjoy investing in vacation real estate. Years ago, we wanted to rent a house on the North Fork of Long Island. I was shocked that rents for even modest homes were in the $5,000 per week range. This prompted me to start looking at properties for sale in the area. I found a charming home with a pool, pond, and tons of privacy that was only a short walk from the beach. Curious to see if my "Albany" positive cash flow model would work, I set about crunching numbers.

No dice. The seasonal rental payments would cover, at best, two-thirds of the monthly mortgage payments and other carrying costs. Unlike the residential rentals, however, this vacation property could also be used and enjoyed by our family in between paying customers. I factored in the money saved that would otherwise be spent renting other people's vacation properties. I then calculated the tax benefits, and most importantly, the internal appreciation in the fair market value of the asset over time.

Ultimately, I pulled the trigger, and count this as one of the best decisions in my life.

Have I ever had a tenant from hell who threw all of my furniture in the pool? No. I credit this to Marie Beninati, MBA, CPA, who is my highly competent real estate broker. She vets prospective tenants, runs credit checks, and takes a very hefty deposit against damage and breakage. Is this worth her healthy rental commission? Without a doubt.

I find it is the investors who try to handle everything on their own—who try to wring the very last dollar from their rentals—who end up frustrated and then sell the property. I am happy to earn a little bit less over a longer period of time—and have fewer headaches.

The mortgage on this property was paid off years ago. It now generates a modest $30,000 annual profit. A portion of the earnings is dedicated to annual additions to boost the rental appeal. New kayaks, bikes, chaise lounges, and super premium beds and linens are all essential.

As an investment, a vacation rental only works for someone who truly enjoys curating a space. Fortunately, I do. Hunting for interesting furniture at estate sales, buying pool toys and games for incoming tenants' children, are all "Quadrant Two" activities for me. I readily confess that I even enjoy cleaning the home. I approach this job from the perspective of an arriving tenant. Someone such as myself, who tentatively looks around and feels totally relieved when there is no "ick" factor.

On more than one occasion, we used the money generated from seasonal rentals to stay in other people's properties. We rented a chateau in the Loire Valley, France, for four weeks with some of our rental proceeds.

More recently, we used the same calculation to buy a newly constructed ski property in Windham, New York. It is more than breaking even financially, while simultaneously serving as a great base from which to engage in many "Quadrant Two" activities such as skiing, hiking, trail-running, and antiquing.

Owning Your Business Real Estate

Self-employed and small business owners should seriously consider working toward owning the property from which they operate. For most business owners, rent is a significant expense. There is a lot to be said for being able to save and invest the money that you would otherwise be paying your landlord. Renting out any space you aren't using is another great income generator. Ideally, your tenant is engaged in a complementary profession to enable cross referrals between businesses.

Service professionals can also use their practices to facilitate the purchase of additional business or office buildings. I unintentionally stumbled upon this model about ten years ago when I fell in love with a small office building. It was constructed in 1895 on Main Street in the former whaling village of Port Jefferson, New York. The office portion had been used for forty years by a realtor, who had recently died. There was an existing residential tenant who occupied the upstairs. The building was pristine. A wood-burning fireplace, original wide-plank maple flooring, high ceilings, built-in bookcases, and original windows are only a few of this property's physical attributes. The ground floor offices were freshly painted.

My lack of renovation skills would not pose a problem. The place was literally turnkey. Budding real estate maven that I thought I was, I had a plan that couldn't fail. The upstairs residential tenant would remain in place. I would then rent out the main floor to three separate but complementary solo practitioners. I was thinking that a real estate broker, an accountant, and a financial advisor would be the ideal tenants. The building's layout would give everyone a separate entrance. With the nearly guaranteed prospects of cross referrals, who would not want to be a tenant here?

Failure was not even a remote possibility, so I pulled the trigger. You can tell that I am headed for trouble, right?

Shortly after the closing, I submitted a permit application to put a new sign out front in place of the deceased real estate broker's sign. My application was denied because the building was only zoned for residential, not commercial or business use. I shrugged this off as a minor technicality and hired a zoning attorney to seek a variance. As of this writing, the legal action has been ongoing for more than ten years. During this time, I have not rented out any office space.

Many well-intentioned people have pointed out that my mistake was seeking a sign permit. I should have simply erected a sign. I guess this is in the category of "better to ask forgiveness than permission."

It turned out that many businesses in this area were operating out of conformity with their residential status. Still a New York State assemblywoman at the time, I felt that I didn't have this luxury. I imagined that ignoring the zoning rules would once again land me in the crosshairs of the *Daily News*.

In any event, I now had a mortgage and carrying costs to pay. There is no special zoning required for an attorney to practice law out of his or her own property. So, I simply announced a new office location to my existing client base. Many of my dear clients helpfully spread the word to friends and relatives in and around Port Jefferson.

Since the time of purchase, I have practiced law from this office one or two days each month. The revenue thus generated, together with the residential rental, has more than covered the carrying costs of this property. I used the excess monthly income to accelerate my mortgage payments, thereby paying it off, many years early.

I recently repeated this model with the purchase of an historic office building in Albany. I am in the process of seeking professional tenants. Unless or until it is fully rented, I will "hang out a shingle" and practice law to the extent needed to cover the building's costs. After all, I know the way to Albany, having served there as a legislator for 14 years.

TAKEAWAYS

- Being in debt robs us of our health, joy, and time spent worrying. Commit today to not taking on even $1 in new debt.
- Sell some stuff around the house and consider a side hustle to generate some money to split between savings and paying down any existing debt.

11

The Laws of Wealth and Generosity

By far, the single most important thing we can do to turbocharge our wealth building is to responsibly share what we have with others. We learned that we should share in preschool.

The overwhelming majority of my clients reported the adoption of generous practices as the mechanism that elevated their levels of wealth and happiness. Many of us plan to become more generous when we hit the next level of wealth. Waiting to be generous, though, can actually delay the next level of wealth. Back to Newton's Third Law—what we put out there comes back to us. Give something away today for an instant mojo boost.

My lottery-winning clients who lost it all reported feelings of selfishness for not having responsibly shared their windfall early on.

The adoption of generous practices is the missing ingredient in most "laws of attraction" or "manifesting" definitions. Think about it: Are the three classic manifesting steps not fundamentally selfish?

1. Get clear about what *you* want.
2. Believe it is on its way to *you*.
3. Act as if *you* already have it.

How can this not strike some part of our brains as wrong? If you believe as I do, that we are fundamentally cooperative beings who evolved to share food and resources with each other, then sitting on a mountain wishing for things won't get us very far. If I invite you to a dinner party, wouldn't your first question be what you can bring?

Instead of focusing ad nauseum on our own wants and needs, we would all be better off to first ask what can we give to others.

"How can I make things better for someone else?" is a question I ask myself several times each day.

No matter how little we currently have, sharing with someone less fortunate provides an immediate energy boost. As a child, my school was collecting food for poor families. I looked through our pantry for a donation. I confess that I grabbed something that I would not miss—a can of Spam. It did feel great to contribute the can to the basket in class next to the nun's desk. Sister Diane took a break from whacking kids to give me a tiny nod of approval. I felt proud and happy to help.

Some days later, my mother answered the door while I was watching TV. It was my friend Sheila's father. How strange . . .

Then I saw it—*a basket of food*! We were one of the poor families that my school was helping. How utterly embarrassing. I hoped with all of my being that Mr. Corbett would not tell Sheila.

The horrors of this moment cannot be overstated. The awful can of Spam even made its way back into the house! I wanted to die. Then, as my mother walked Mr. Corbett out, I noticed something in the basket. It was the corner of a brown shiny bag. This was too good to be true, but the shade of brown was unmistakable. It was a big bag of miniature Snickers bars! I was euphoric—and very selfish. I grabbed the bag and hid it in my closet before anyone else could see it.

The Snickers bars seemed to last forever and made me happier than anything had as of that point in my life. This continues to be one of my fondest memories. I thought about the person (I learned later that this angel was my social studies teacher, Juliette VanBellinghen) who was wonderful enough to imagine a child on the receiving end of the donation. I learned the power of being an agent of change in someone else's life. I learned the magic of giving someone else a little boost and the positive events that a wonderful surprise can set into motion. I clearly remember vowing to do this for other people once I could.

I try to incorporate sharing into my daily life. I never miss a chance to donate to groups organizing food drives. Trying to pay forward the magic of my Snickers windfall, I always include some purely fun donations. On a recent trip to a food pantry, I brought three bags of Snickers and three bags of Milky Ways. Later in the day, I got a phone call from the food pantry organizer. She thanked me for my donations but wished to discuss some fundamentals of nutritious eating with me. She would be unable to give my bags of candy to families in need!

I told her that I have it on very good authority that poor kids like treats too. Canned beans, vegetables, pasta, and the like, are undoubtedly essential. I get where she was coming from. However, I know for a fact that inspired and whimsical generosity can create magic.

Generous Actions Come Back to Us

There is a famous legend about a poor Scottish farmer named Fleming. One day, while toiling in the fields, he heard a child crying for help. He dropped what he was doing and ran to the bog next to his barn. He jumped in to save a young boy flailing about from near certain drowning. The following day, the young boy's father came back to the farm to compensate Mr. Fleming for saving his son. The farmer stated that anyone would have done the same and refused any gift from the well-dressed man. At some point during the brief exchange, the farmer's son appeared and greeted the well-turned-out visitor.

The visitor was moved to insist that he provide an education for the farmer's son equal to that afforded to his own son. Unable to refuse such a tremendous advantage for his son, the farmer agreed. The boy was brought to London where he resided with the benefactor and his son while he completed his education. Farmer Fleming's son eventually graduated from St. Mary's Hospital Medical School. He would later be known to the world as Dr. Alexander Fleming, who discovered penicillin, thereby saving the lives of countless people.

Sadly, there is no historical support for this lovely tale. That, however, did not stop me from sharing it often with my kids' bedtime stories. It illustrates the potential ripple effect of generous actions.

Wild Spending on Ourselves Repels Wealth

I learned from my windfall recipient clients that spending money like a drunken sailor without protecting and responsibly sharing it is a guaranteed prescription for misery and poverty. Failure to responsibly share doesn't mean that they refused to share. In fact, most windfall recipients shared too much of their wealth. They just didn't do it responsibly.

Indiscriminately handing out fistfuls of cash, so that friends, family, and hangers-on can buy expensive toys is not a worthwhile proposition. Remember, no matter how much we give to cousin Fred, it will never be enough. He will not stop asking until you finally say no or you have nothing left to give. Cousin Fred will not appreciate what you gave him. In all likelihood, once you say no or the money is gone, then so too will be the relationship.

Responsibly Sharing Creates a Belief That All Things Are Possible

Humans are social creatures. We are hardwired and naturally selected to live and work in groups. Those of our ancestors who were part of groups cooperatively sharing responsibilities and resources were more likely than the loners to live and procreate. Those alive today have evolved to share resources with others. Based on my interviews of thousands of clients seeking wealth protection, I know that sharing what we have with others gives today's humans benefits far beyond mere survival. We can literally transform and elevate our own lives by responsibly sharing what we have—right now, with others.

Generous acts are a natural consequence of our capacity to empathize with others. We become aware of the many needs of members of our human family. When we see need, instead of turning the channel or newspaper page or scrolling past it on our phone screen, we might instead give some thought to how we might be of help.

This mindset shift does a few things. First, it gets us out of some well-worn mental loops about what we don't have and what's not working in our own lives. The mindset shift toward helping others also proves to the tiny judge that sits in our heads that we have the ability to change others' circumstances.

Having the ability and desire to positively change circumstances is my personal definition of happiness. Lifting others up proves that we have transformative power. This is the only way to hone the elusive belief that there are generous and benevolent forces in the universe. Why wouldn't some of these forces seek expression in our own lives?

Again, Newton's Third Law tells us that what we put out there in the world can't help but come back to us. This law is as absolute as gravity. If I drop a rubber ball, it will bounce back up. If I push my hand into a loaf of Wonder Bread, it will decompress and reach back toward me.

If we help others, we will be helped. This reciprocal nature of generosity is the essence of the Golden Rule. Treat others as we wish to be treated.

Generosity at Work

People who share credit for their work with colleagues report magical results. When dealing with a junior colleague, application of the Golden Rule should cause us to treat him or her the way we wish we had been treated as we were coming up the ranks. By giving "Irene" credit—not only to her face, but also to colleagues, when she isn't present—we immediately elevate ourselves in the estimation of everyone around us.

Most importantly, the little judge who lives in our brain sees this. Our self-esteem and belief that we are deserving of good things to come, will be turbocharged. Refusal to speak ill of a colleague will cause everyone around us to trust that we will not speak ill of them. They will trust us, and we will thereby rise in their esteem. If my coworkers think well of me and speak well of me, that is worth one million times more than sole credit for any given project.

Personal growth master Zig Ziglar advised that we can get whatever we want in life, if only we help enough other people get what they want. Lifting others up is a surefire gateway to our next level up!

Generous Teams Excel

If there is one single practice that can almost instantly capture and implement the foregoing principles, it is a group charitable project. Ideally, all the participants get to nominate and advocate for a given charitable endeavor. The entire team then votes for the winner.

One of our annual office projects is "Valentines for Veterans." We create and collect cards, treats, toiletries, puzzles, and other games for our hospitalized heroes. Team members, clients, and the community at-large come in to add their heartfelt contributions to the big heart-festooned box in our reception area. Watching each other cut and paste construction paper hearts instantly helps dispel petty annoyances. We feel more like a team and more like we can accomplish positive results in the greater community. How can this not boost morale and help business?

By adopting a generous spirit and thinking about what we can do to help junior colleagues, we prove to ourselves that willing help and support exists. We also prove to ourselves that we are deserving of good things. By helping others reach the next level, we step into a network of supportive forces. By generously sharing our talents, expertise, and encouragement, we strengthen and broaden the foundation from which we can all soar. This goes far in developing a real belief that we will benefit from external forces to support our own efforts to reach our ultimate goals.

Givers Gain

Legendary personal development expert and philosopher Bob Proctor advises us that "Givers Gain." This is so true. Generosity is reciprocal.

In her book *Giving Is Not Just for the Very Rich*, philanthropist Dr. Susan Gitelson promises that "the more you give to others, the happier you are likely to become."

What are the physical and material elements of the object of your definite desire? Do you lust after a new home? In addition to visualizing and working toward it, you may wish to help someone else improve their physical shelter. By deploying some of your current resources and efforts to those who need them, you will be an agent of change.

It has been said that the things we crave most in life are achieved by giving them to someone else. Do you think this makes you more or less likely to receive positive change in your own life?

Is it wrong to engage in charitable efforts, if part of our motivation is a desire to improve our own circumstances? If we pose this question to the person or family that we are helping, I am guessing that they will give us a thumbs up!

As I write this, my son, Billy Duke, is volunteering at a Los Angeles-area soup kitchen. I know with every fiber of my being that his chief motivation in doing so is to meet celebrities who are also volunteering there (whether on the recommendation of a publicist or a court-ordered parole condition). His motivation is secondary to any help that he can provide to folks in need, but I am confident that by sharing company with generous people as well as those with needs, he will develop empathy and a true desire to help others.

It is a fact, supported by every world faith tradition, that we humans are happier when we share (responsibly) what we have with others. A few examples:

> "Good will come to him who is generous."
> —Psalm 112:5

> "Gain all you can, Save all you can and Give all you can."
> —John Wesley, founder of Methodism

Why, then, do so many people not incorporate sharing into their lives?

I believe the answer is that we are afraid. We fear not having enough resources for ourselves and our immediate families. A lot of clients tell me that they will gladly share—once they have enough to do so. Sounds somewhat reasonable. The problem, though, is that failing to share our existing resources, modest though they may be, may actually be keeping us poor.

Fear of becoming poor is understandable. Again, no amount of wealth is infinite. It is only by employing methods to actively grow and legally protect what we currently have that we can repel the fear of losing it all. Banishing the fear of loss should free us up to responsibly share. Unleashing the magic of sharing will, in turn, cause more wealth to come our way.

My three pillars of wealth—growing, protecting, and responsibly sharing—really are interdependent. If I have objective proof that my savings are growing, I will be less susceptible to the fear of loss. Putting regular simultaneous effort into the three areas of the wealth plan cannot fail to produce powerful results.

I believe that generous acts can help us to attract wealth. Being selfish repels wealth. Before looking more closely at this, however, I think it is instructive to look at a condition worse than selfishness. If responsibly sharing whatever we happen to have at the moment is the gold standard for enlightenment and happiness, and if being a selfish miser is an express train to misery (*miser* is the root of misery), there is a condition that is worse still. That is taking money from others by way of theft, fraud, and unfair bargains.

The Opposite of Generosity Is Theft

An eye-popping number of people surveyed admit to having stolen merchandise or money from employers. Are we hardwired to steal? Were our ancestors who made sure to eat, whether it was their own food or that of a neighbor's, more likely to live long enough to reproduce? Perhaps.

Evolutionary underpinnings notwithstanding, theft of workplace resources is extremely damaging to the entire community. The act of stealing is the clearest possible proof to the little judge who lives in our heads that we are undeserving of good things. It is simply not possible to believe we deserve wonderful things if we are thieves. This is why countless white-collar criminals express some sense of relief upon being caught.

There can be no justification for theft of time or resources. Your boss may well be a pinhead. However, surfing the internet instead of working for two hours will harm you more than it will harm your boss. This will sap you of self-esteem, which will in turn, erode your belief that good things are in your future. As Ralph Waldo Emerson said, "The thief steals from himself."

The restaurant business is said to be rife with employee theft. I make it a point to ask my restaurateur clients about this. When I ask restaurant owners how they prevent employees from stealing, one hundred percent of them gave me the exact same answer: that it is impossible to prevent theft. The only real goal, they tell me, is to prevent their employees from becoming fifty-fifty partners in the business.

When I worked at Dunkin' Donuts as a 16-year-old, I remember noticing an employee who would collect the customer's money, hit the "open" cash register button, and give the customer his or her change. One teeny tiny detail, though, was omitted. The actual sale was not entered into the register. I later learned that this person would keep track of the "unentered" money, and later enter it into his pocket! The price he paid for these few extra dollars ended up being a criminal record.

When I worked in retail, there were numerous safeguards against employee theft. Most of the procedures were downright insulting. Macy's Herald Square had a separate employee door, through which everyone had to exit, only after being searched by a security guard! Still, I remember more than a few arrests of coworkers who managed to steal clothes.

If the goal of the thief was to have extra money or clothes, there were far better methods of attaining both. The only limit on one's financial upside is the belief you deserve wealth. Stealing hobbles true wealth creation by giving your mind instant and irrefutable proof that you are not deserving of it.

If failing to share causes sadness for the miser, what does theft cause for the criminal? Like watching a car crash, I am intrigued and drawn to stories of white-collar crime. I am not sure that

I've ever picked up a copy of the *New York Law Journal* without reading about an attorney losing his or her license to practice law because of an escrow-account violation.

This story is a very familiar one. The attorney is living beyond his means and feels tremendous pressure to meet payment obligations. At the same time, he happens to have unfettered access to a client's money, which he is supposed to be holding inviolate by way of the escrow account. These monies are usually the result of a court settlement or real estate purchase being temporarily held back until some legal requirement is satisfied.

Invasion of the escrow accounts is a problem that must go back a long way. Anyone who has taken the bar exam knows the emphasis each state places on inculcating soon-to-be attorneys with the sacrosanct nature of funds that are entrusted to you for your client's benefit. Part of the bar exam in all states is the "MPRE." This is the multistate professional responsibility exam. More than one-half of the questions seemed to focus on escrow account protections: "True or False, should you take money from your client's escrow account if you intend to repay it?" "Should you take money from your client's escrow account to prevent your home from being foreclosed upon?" There seemed to be no limit on the variations of that question. Yet, every day, attorneys do, in fact, raid their clients' escrow accounts.

Early on in my private law practice, I was encouraged by professional colleagues to install cameras in the office. The goal being to deter and detect theft of office supplies and hours lost to spider solitaire and online dating. I opted not to install cameras. I choose, instead, to try to foster an environment where people feel valued.

Is it inevitable that some people will steal office supplies? Probably. I do what I can, though, not to put them in this position. Each August, for example, I invite all parents to fulfill their kids' school supply lists through our office supply account.

Long before I had anything of material value to share, I still wanted to give people surprises. I would draw pictures and leave them in neighbors' mailboxes. On one occasion, "Old Lady" Halperin (her real name!) screamed at me through her window that tampering with a mailbox was a federal offense and I would go to prison. She was taken off of my distribution list. All other recipients were dutifully appreciative of my low-talent renderings.

TAKEAWAYS

- Surprising others with generous actions will produce magic for both the giver and the recipient.
- Being generous does not have to cost money, so you don't have to wait until you are flush to start being an agent of change.
- Taking a genuine interest in your colleagues' lives will shift your work atmosphere.

12
Generosity in Your Estate Plan

Thoughtful estate planning gives us the opportunity to maximize what ends up going to our surviving loved ones, while simultaneously sparing them frustration, confusion, and acrimony.

Is your family the same as every other family you know? Of course not. Why, then, would you want to have the exact same will? I bet that many of those reading this that have wills all have the same document. This utterly fails to take into consideration the (ahem) complexities within our respective realities. Failure to customize will result in the loss of estate assets.

We customize every other area of our lives. Whoever would have thought, forty years ago, that we would have such a dizzying array of water, coffee, jeans, or sneaker choices?

One day, people will be in disbelief at the notion that everyone used to use the same exact will or trust template. The first step to putting this clumsy practice in the rearview mirror is to identify potentially costly life situations.

Second Marriages

Recall from our earlier discussion that the divorce rate for second and subsequent marriages is higher than 60 percent! A financially devastating divorce is a particularly hard blow for people with fewer working years ahead. Chances that one of the parties will need costly long-term health care are near 80 percent. Medicare does not cover this care. Spouses are financially responsible for each other's health care expenses. Chances that one or both of the parties will have children are high. Chances that the parties' children will hate each other are perhaps even higher. Mix these factors together, and the need for some customization in the estate plan should be obvious.

At a minimum, those embarking upon or in a second marriage should create a prenup or postnup (discussed in chapter 4 and chapter 5). Next, decide whether to appoint a spouse or adult child as our health care proxy or power of attorney. Who do we want making our decisions in the event of a cognitive impairment? Saying that we will wait until later to deal with this is silly. Waiting to create these documents until there is a problem may render them legally void. That's why they are called "advance directives." They must be created in advance of an impairment.

Failure to create a health care proxy or power of attorney can lead the family to an extremely expensive court proceeding. This is called a guardianship or conservatorship proceeding. I recommend that you avoid this at all costs. Imagine your spouse and children fighting in court over who is best positioned to make health care and financial decisions for you.

Britney Spears was in her twenties when a court determined that she needed a conservator. Because there were no advance directives in place, whereby Ms. Spears could have appointed the person of her choice to take over in the event of incapacity, the court appointed the singer's father. Britney Spears was to spend the following thirteen years and untold millions of dollars arguing that he was not the person that she wanted in the role.

We don't always get advance warning that we will be out of commission. Put some structures in place now to help your loved ones smoothly and economically handle things if you become unable to. Start with a free health care proxy on mylawyerann.com. This action step will create positive momentum!

Gifts and Loans to Loved Ones

If you have made a gift or a loan to a loved one, please acknowledge this in your estate plan. If I loan $100,000 to my daughter and she never gets around to repaying it, there will be costly wrangling with her siblings after my death. They will want to reduce her share of the estate to reflect the $100,000. She will likely say it was a gift and therefore has no bearing on the equal distribution of my remaining estate.

A one-size-fits-all estate plan cannot adequately prevent explosive and expensive family warfare later. One "fill-in-the-blanks" company boasts that your estate plan can be created in less time than it takes to order a pizza! This may be cheaper up front, but it is not a generous action for loved ones later.

MEET THE ACERTO FAMILY

Peggy is a widow with three adult children. Her son, Joey, manages the family's card store. He is single and is financially stable. His sister Jennifer is married with two children. She owns her home but is treading water financially. The third child, Melissa, is a financial train wreck. She is separated from her second husband and has moved back to her mother's house with her two high-school-age children. Peggy is funding the legal fees for the current divorce.

Peggy has a very simple will which was done before the death of her husband years ago. The problem with the will is not how long ago it was created. The problem is its failure to address some potential financial fault lines between the three children. I meet with clients like Peggy on a weekly basis. She wants to keep things simple. She thinks a trust is only for super wealthy people. She is also reluctant to delve too deeply into what will happen upon her death, because she doesn't want to think about it. Fear of death causes many of us to shrink away from making thoughtful arrangements to protect our loved ones. This type of person can barely summon the resolve to come into my office and ask for a simple will.

When I try to elicit a deeper dialogue, Peggy shuts down. Responses include: "They will work it out," or the classic "what will it matter—I won't be here"; also "they should be glad they are getting anything" and "do you know what my parents left me?"

Upon Peggy's death, the backdrop is set for World War III. The assets consist of the house worth $600,000, the business worth $200,000, and cash in the bank of $100,000. Who thinks that a three-way even distribution is fair? Certainly not the three Acerto children.

Even though on paper there is $300,000 in value for each of the three siblings, the road to that point will be rocky. Joey was told by his mother that the business would be his. Melissa was told that she and the kids could stay in the house as long as needed. She was also assured that her mother would fund all of the divorce legal fees. Jennifer just wants the estate assets to be sold quickly. She has been counting on this money.

Did Peggy actually believe it when she said that her kids would amicably work everything out? I don't think she even really thought it through. She dreaded the thought of her mortality and was unable to give nuanced attention to her children's future.

Egged on by their respective close friends, Joey, Jennifer, and Melissa all hire attorneys to safeguard their rights. Jennifer's attorney demands that income from the card shop be split three ways until the business is sold. Joey's attorney wants to list the family home for sale. He also wants Melissa to pay fair market value rent going back to the date she first moved in with Peggy. The only thing that Joey's and Melissa's attorneys agree upon is that Jennifer's share of the estate should be reduced by $100,000 because of a loan the parents gave her as a down payment on her home ten years ago.

Before Peggy's death, the three siblings were extremely close. They did not spontaneously wake up one day hating each other. Instead, through no fault of their own, they find themselves pitted against each other. They are each driven by a deep fear for their ability to survive financially. The stage is set for a lengthy legal battle which will bring out the worst qualities in all three. It is probable that their relationships will be forever damaged. They are in this situation for one reason. Peggy failed to anticipate fault lines and create some legal guardrails to protect her children. They are now desperately frightened for their financial security. Ironically, they will all walk away with much less, after hefty legal fees are paid.

If my son "Bobby" is 57 years old and has not saved $5 toward his retirement, it would be reckless for me to leave him one-third of my estate in an unprotected fashion. When I urge parents with a Bobby on the scene to create a protective trust to hold, manage, and administer his share of the estate, I hear a universal objection: "I don't want to hurt his feelings."

Could this be an extension of the parenting style that allowed Bobby to have as many Twinkies as he wanted as a child? There are probably multiple reasons that Bobby hasn't held a job for years and spends all day on the couch watching TV. It does not matter what those reasons are. It doesn't matter whether they are his fault or someone else's fault.

What kind of favor am I doing for my son, by allowing him to blow through his share of my estate in no time flat? Will he be insulted that his share of the estate is in a protective trust? Maybe. Isn't this short-lived insult when the will is read, though, preferable to him having no roof over his head within a year of the inheritance? Without a trust in place, where will Bobby turn after he has blown through or been tricked out of his inheritance?

His brother and sister, of course! Bobby will badger them for money, until those relationships are destroyed. Again, I caution you that one-size-fits-all estate planning generally fits no one. Assets will be eroded, and beneficiaries will be pitted against each other. What kind of gift is that?

We know the strengths and weaknesses of our loved ones. I urge you to consider implementing the structures discussed earlier to protect those closest to your heart. A thoughtfully crafted estate plan will increase the total amount of assets gifted while ensuring that they will stretch out as long as possible.

Planning for Youngsters and Money

Parents of minor children must appoint guardians for them within a validly created and executed will. Failure to do this can cause heartache for everyone involved. As with many aspects of legal planning, when we fail to make a decision, our state legislature makes one for us. Failure to legally appoint a guardian for children on a will leaves it up to a judge.

Please don't let this happen. The court proceeding here is to be avoided at all costs. Family members will be pitted against each other, thereby damaging the support network the children so desperately need at this time. Moreover, the legal fees involved will be eye-popping. They will greatly reduce assets in your estate that would otherwise pass to your children. It is not enough that you had a verbal conversation with family members. Nor is it enough that you wrote down your guardian selection on a piece of paper stored with your important documents. The I's must be dotted and the T's must be crossed within a validly executed will.

I understand that this decision is perhaps the hardest one to make. I don't know any parents, myself included, who aren't reduced to tears at the thought of someone else raising our children. Failure to deal with this, though, may cause years of anguish for the people you love most in the world. My advice here is not to let the perfect be the enemy of the good. Of course, there is no perfect guardian for your children. Better, though, to appoint a good guardian, than to leave this critically important decision in limbo.

If you are truly uncomfortable at the prospect of naming anyone in your life as the sole guardian, you may consider naming two people to act jointly. If these two people are not in the same household, you can leave the decision up to them to determine whose home the children will live in. Joint guardianship ensures that two people have input into all medical, educational, and other life decisions for the kids.

Alternatively, we can split the role of guardian into the roles of primary caregiver and custodian or trustee of the money. Let's say, for example, that my sister is a preschool teacher. She is warm, nurturing, and loving. I would trust her with my life as well as the lives of my precious little ones. I know that she would create a fun and supportive environment for my children. What should I do, though, if I also know that she is a total disaster with money?

If my goal is to protect whatever assets I've managed to accumulate as of my date of death, for the benefit of my children, I should not put a financial train wreck in charge of the money. This is inviting a financial disaster.

Instead, I can appoint my sister as guardian "of the person." She will then have day-to-day caregiving responsibilities as well as physical custody of the children. What about the money? We should name a trustee of our children's money.

The number-one mistake I see, on a weekly basis, involves the manner in which folks attempt to leave money and other assets to children and grandchildren. If you have youngsters in your life, it is statistically likely that you have named them as beneficiaries or backup beneficiaries on your financial accounts. There is a one hundred percent chance that this is a costly mistake. Why is this?

The answer is found in a sad but true story of a child actor from one hundred years ago. Jackie Coogan was a wildly successful child star. His movies served as a temporary respite from the ravages of the Great Depression for our grandparents and great grandparents. They also catapulted little Jackie to international fame. He was, through the better part of his childhood and adolescence, one of the most famous people in the United States.

When Jackie turned twenty-one, he expected to finally take possession of the enormous sums of money he earned over the years. There was just one problem. His mother and stepfather spent every cent of the estimated $4 million fortune! There was nothing left.

Young Jackie lawyered up and sued his mother and stepfather for the blown assets. His mother argued that a child's money legally belongs to parents prior to the age of twenty-one. She, therefore, had no duty to safeguard the money for Jackie's future.

The practical problem, of course, was that there was nothing left. Even if the mother had been ordered by a court to return the money, she had no ability to do so. This was a riveting case that made headlines nationwide and led to the enactment of laws in every state designed to protect the money of youngsters from possible evildoers, which now included parents.

Every parent and grandparent needs to be aware of these laws. Eileen and Ron were not.

Eileen and Ron were the proud parents of 43-year-old Brooke and grandparents of her sons Darren, 14, and David, 11.

Eileen and Ron's estate planning consisted of simple wills that left everything to each other and then whatever remained upon the death of the survivor was to be divided equally between Darren and David. They bypassed Brooke because they hated her husband, Marvin.

In an effort to prevent the family from having to probate their wills, they had, wherever possible, named the boys as direct beneficiaries on their various financial holdings. Their life insurance, bank accounts, and retirement accounts all listed each other as primary beneficiary and the children as the backup or contingent beneficiary.

What Eileen and Ron didn't realize is that children cannot legally own things. Furthermore, Brooke, as their mother, had no automatic rights to oversee the money until the children reached the age of majority (this is either eighteen or twenty-one years old, depending upon your state of residence). This is because the laws of every state seek to protect children from the fate of Jackie Coogan.

So, when Eileen and Ron died in a boating accident, a court saga ensued. None of the banks or brokerage firms would release funds to the kids or to their mother, absent a court order. Brooke hired a lawyer to petition the court for such an order.

In cases like this, the court appoints a stranger, known as a *guardian ad litem*, to oversee the investment and protection of the assets until the children are adults. Do you think that the court-appointed guardian undertakes this role on a *pro bono* or volunteer basis?

Absolutely not! These plum assignments pay well, by way of an annual commission, which is a percentage of the children's money. In addition, the law allows the guardians to be reimbursed for their expenses. Do they need to meet with the accountant and financial advisor for the money? Sure. Do these meetings need to take place over (multiple) steak dinners with cocktails? No, but they will likely get away with this.

Unless, of course, Brooke wants to spend more in legal fees to challenge the guardian's annual accounting (paid for out of the children's money). Given the fact that judges give these coveted roles to their friends and former political supporters, any financial misdeeds would have to be pretty egregious for a court to intervene.

I understand the logical and visceral appeal of naming youngsters as beneficiaries. However, this is yet another example of how trying to keep things simple causes massive hemorrhaging of assets down the road.

What should Eileen and Ron have done? If their goal was to bypass their daughter, Brooke, for any reason, they should have considered creating . . . yes, you guessed it—a trust!

Protective Trusts for Our Little Loved Ones

Again, the worst way to leave assets to a youngster is to name them as a direct beneficiary on any account. A slightly better, though still bad, method is to name the youngsters in a will, with some language providing that the named executor safeguard the assets until the child is twenty-one.

This method is somewhat better because it will prevent the court from appointing a stranger to oversee the money. It is still bad, though, because nothing in the will can take effect without a full-blown probate.

Instead, we should create a separate trust for the young people in our lives. This is what I have for my children. This can be a single trust, designed to administer assets for the benefit of several youngsters, or a separate trust for each child. Note that this trust can be revocable.

Yes, I did caution you not to rely on a Revocable trust to protect assets. In this case, however, I am not funding the trust with significant assets. In fact, I typically have clients fund this trust with just $10. However, because the trust is created during my life and is technically funded during my life, we can apply for a separate tax ID number for it. The trust now meets all of the requirements to be a valid beneficiary on bank accounts and other financial instruments.

Once this young person's trust is created, I will call my insurance agent. After dashing his hopes that I am not calling to buy more insurance, I should ask him for a change of beneficiary form. I will then simply fill the form out, changing the named beneficiary from little Johnny to "Johnny Lopez Trust, dated, 2/14/2025." Think of this trust as a snap-on Lego piece that can be inserted as a beneficiary anywhere that an individual beneficiary could be named.

This method is far superior because I am free to customize the manner in which assets paid to the trust (upon my death) are held, managed, invested, and ultimately paid out to the child or children. This will prevent death benefits from being paid to a youngster, which would cause a court to "oversee" the monies.

One of the most important areas for customization is the age at which the young beneficiary can actually receive their trust assets. Here, I encourage you to hold the assets back as long as possible. Anything below the age of twenty-five is usually a mistake. Yes, I know that you want the money to be used for college. The best way to do this, though, is to keep the money in the trust.

Think about it. If the money can legally belong to the child at eighteen or even twenty-one years old, then these assets will count against Junior when he applies for college financial aid. This hypothetical $10,000 will result in $10,000 less in terms of financial aid that he may otherwise have qualified for. Wouldn't we prefer that he have the benefit of maximum financial aid together with his trust assets?

Junior can have his cake and eat it too if the assets remain in trust, to be held, managed, and administered until he is twenty-five.

In the meantime, though, the named trustee (I will be the initially named trustee, but the person I have named as the backup will take control upon my death or earlier incapacity) has the discretion to use trust assets for any number of purposes that I wish to designate, *including education*.

Why am I giving the trustee discretion when this is my number-one goal with the money? Well, if it is within the trustee's discretion, he or she is not required to use money in the trust for Junior's college. If they aren't required, then Junior does not have to list the trust assets on the all-important college financial aid application forms!

He will, therefore, qualify for maximum financial aid. The trustee can then use the trust assets to add to this. Now, he has the benefit of whatever college financial aid is available together with what I've left him in the trust.

Choosing a higher-than-average age to receive assets will enable them to last longer. We can do even better, though, in terms of protecting the assets, if we choose three separate ages to receive staggered portions of what's in the trust. My trust says that my children receive their interests upon my death, "provided that they take legal steps to keep inherited assets separate from whatever they may choose to comingle with a spouse or partner."

However, if, at the time of my death, anyone is younger than thirty-five, the trustee will hold back what they otherwise would have received. Instead, the trustee will distribute one-third to the child at age twenty-five, half of what's left at thirty, and the full distribution at thirty-five. Prior to these stated ages, the trustee can use assets for anything that the child may need. This trust can even buy a home or condo for the child.

The staggered distribution approach gives the named beneficiary three separate chances to responsibly manage the inheritance. This better protects the child from the consequences of bad investment decisions or ill-advised marriage.

Beneficiaries with Special Needs

If there is a child or adult in your life who has a developmental disability or other chronic condition unlikely to change, then we need to consider a different type of trust. A so-called Special or Supplemental Needs Trust (SNT) is recognized in all 50 states. This vehicle enables my special loved one to benefit from my assets without them supplanting means-tested program benefits, to which he, she, or they would otherwise be eligible. The trustee of the SNT has the discretion to use trust assets to pay for things not otherwise covered by government programs. This is another method of enabling loved ones to have their cake and eat it too.

The most common way of dealing with beneficiaries with special needs, is the worst way. Parents and grandparents of "differently abled" loved ones appreciate that thought must be given to the estate planning. Unfortunately, the thought usually begins and ends with excluding the person from the will or trust.

MEET JACK AND IRENE

Jack and Irene were the happy parents of Carl and Joey. Joey is on the autism spectrum. He is non-verbal, but near genius level when it comes to math. Joey lives in a group home. He spends his days solving cryptoquotes and memorizing numbers in the phone book. He has been on his state's Medicaid program since he turned 18.

Jack and Irene knew that they should not give or leave Joey significant assets, at the risk of jeopardizing his eligibility for "means-tested" government programs such as Medicaid. Instead, they did what 99 percent of parents in this situation mistakenly do. You guessed it. They left everything to Carl, because they "knew he would always do the right thing by his brother."

They were right about Carl. After Jack and Irene died, Carl always made sure that his brother had the "extras" not covered by his government program benefits. These included puzzle books, new pajamas, sheets, and pocket money for pizza and the movies.

Life was to throw Joey another curve ball. Carl died. Carl followed his parents' lead by not including Joey in his will. Instead, he left his entire estate to his wife, Belinda. Within a year, she was remarried. Unfortunately for Joey, she never took an interest in him. For whatever reason, she never visited him and never ventured to buy him anything or give him pocket money. Joey's remaining years were decidedly less enjoyable because every member of his family dropped the legal ball.

This is another classic example of a disaster resulting from a misguided attempt to keep things simple within the estate plan. How easy would it have been for Jack and Irene to create a special needs trust? They could have funded it with a nominal $20 and acquired a separate tax ID Number. Their wills (and trust for their home, if they had been enlightened) could have provided that 80 percent of their estate go to Carl and 20 percent go directly to Joey's trust. Provided that the SNT is properly drafted, it will not interfere with program benefits. It will, however, enable the Trustee to buy things for the benefit of the person with special needs that are not otherwise covered by program benefits. In Joey's case, this would have enabled him to continue happily enjoying his puzzle books and treats.

Furry Loved Ones

The 68 percent of Americans with pets would be very well advised to give them some legal protections within their estate plans.

Failure to take some proactive legal steps on the front end will leave your pets to the whim of chance upon your future possible illness and death. Lack of a plan here will also place a tremendous burden on your executor to come up with a thoughtful solution in a hurry.

Many are unaware of the legal pet planning options available today. This ignorance results not only in a lack of protection for existing pets, but also actually prevents many pets from being adopted in the first place. I have heard from more than a few elderly clients that they do not have a pet because they feel that the pet will live longer than they will. Therefore, they express fear about leaving pet orphans to fend for themselves upon their death.

This is really sad on two levels. Studies across the board demonstrate that we are happier, have lower stress, and live longer when we have a pet in the house. Moreover, some pets can protect elderly folks living alone from being victimized by crime. Ignorance about pet planning options reduces the quality of life for some seniors. At the same time, failure to learn of planning options deprives untold numbers of shelter pets of a loving home.

What are these planning options? Glad you asked!

It is not legally possible to leave assets directly to a pet within a will or trust. In the same way that we need to use a specific type of trust to protect assets that we would otherwise wish to leave to a minor child, we need to use a special type of trust as the vehicle through which our pets can benefit from our estate.

All 50 states permit the use of "pet care appointee" (PCA) trusts. This structure allows me to allocate a certain amount of money and give it to a human PCA for the future use and benefit of the furry loved one(s). The PCA may or may not have physical custody of the pet. They would, however, be responsible for securing a suitable home and thereafter ensuring that the pet receives medical care, proper nutrition, and recreation. It is advisable to name a backup PCA who can step in if the primary agent is, for any reason, not able to carry out the mission.

In terms of the amount of money that should be earmarked, my rule of thumb is to multiply your annual food, grooming, and vet bills by the number of years left in your pet's statistical life expectancy. This is the minimum.

The stickier question is how to compensate the PCA? There are two options. The first is to give your agent an annual commission or salary. The second option is to provide that the PCA receive any funds left upon the future death of the pet. Both methods are, to some extent, dependent upon the honor of the named agent.

Let's say that I name my cousin, Kate, as PCA for my canary, Topaz.

My PCA trust provides that Kate receives $6,000 per year in compensation. Upon Topaz's death, the trust ends and any remaining monies are to go to a bird sanctuary. Is there room for Kate to manipulate the situation if she is less than honorable? Absolutely.

Upon the death of Topaz, she can buy a replacement canary, in order to keep her annual salary in place. This can theoretically continue until the trust funds are exhausted.

Alternatively, instead of giving my PCA an annual salary or commission, my PCA trust might provide the agent with a lump sum payment upon the death of the pet. I'm sure you can see how this might tragically be manipulated.

In *Love & Money*, I shared the story of a PCA trust established for seven cats. Upon the death of the last cat, all remaining funds and a New York City condo were to be given to the named PCA. All seven cats were mysteriously dead within two years of their pet parent.

If you have any doubts about the ability of those in your life to resist the financial temptations presented by the foregoing two PCA compensation models, you may wish to involve a reputable not-for-profit organization in the plan. The not-for-profit might be tasked with periodically checking on the pet and ensuring that primary and preventive veterinary care is up to date.

Alternatively, a number of my clients designate a not-for-profit as the PCA. In exchange for taking physical custody and ensuring that every need of the pet is met, the not-for-profit is entitled to any funds remaining in the trust upon the death of the pet. They, in turn, agree to continue caring for the pet even if the funds are exhausted prior to the pet's death.

Thorough pet planning should also cover arrangements during an illness or hospitalization of the pet parent. It is advisable to research short-term pet accommodations in your area. Your veterinarian's office may have good suggestions. You would then give this information to the person you have designated as your agent under the health care proxy. This is the person most likely to be on the scene in the event of an illness or period of incapacity.

Improving the World through Our Estate Plans

There are tax benefits for well-planned charitable giving. The specifics depend on a variety of factors. I encourage you to explore the benefits with your tax adviser and financial adviser as well as the planned giving team of your intended charity.

New York State, for example, has a tricky estate tax system. If an estate is even slightly over the current estate tax threshold ($7.16 million in 2025), then the *entire* estate is subject to tax. This so-called cliff can be avoided with a flexible charitable clause along these lines: "If any portion of my estate exceeds the federal and/or state tax exemption, then I give that amount to [a nonprofit charity, e.g., the American Red Cross]."

The overwhelming majority of my clients express a desire to help their favorite causes early in our planning process. By the time that the ultimate wills and trusts are signed, however, only about ten percent of folks actually make provisions for charities. Why is this?

Yes, people want their favorite charities to benefit. When we get down to decision time, however, most people are profoundly concerned that their primary beneficiaries won't have enough. This is a matter of deeply personal choice. My limited role here is to present clients with options.

One attractive compromise option involves estate tax planning. When our estate value at death exceeds the federal and/or state (where applicable) wealth thresholds in effect at that time (please visit my website for current information: mylawyerann.com), taxes are imposed. Under current law, otherwise taxable estates get to deduct bequests to charities. When I am working with someone whose net worth exceeds the current estate tax threshold, I ask if they would prefer to benefit the US Treasury or their favorite charity. It should not come as a surprise that no one chooses US Treasury.

The problem is that we don't know for sure in advance how much our estate will be worth, nor do we know what the tax laws will be at the time. A hedge against future unknowns is to create a formula within the estate planning. We essentially provide that any part of our estate, which would otherwise trigger estate tax liability on the state and/or federal level, instead go to the ASPCA, St. Jude, or other charity of choice.

There is another compromise possibility for estates below the applicable estate tax thresholds. We can say, "I give my entire estate to Mary, Susie, and Vinny, on the condition that they take steps to keep assets inherited from me separate from those that they choose to comingle with a spouse or partner, and with the hope that they will consider making a donation, in my memory, to [a nonprofit charity, e.g., Feeding America]."

Using the word "hope" leaves the ultimate decision up to the child. This enables them to keep the money if, in fact, they are in need. However, if they choose to make the hoped-for donation, they will likely benefit from an income tax deduction for the charitable gift. Note that there would have been no estate tax benefit if the charitable donation was made directly from the (non-taxable) estate.

Consider Getting Involved in a Grassroots Organization

A few years ago, I became acquainted with Penny's Flight Foundation (PFF). This organization was started in the living room of Kate and Chad Doerge after losing their sixteen-year-old daughter, Penny, to neurofibromatosis (NF), a genetic disorder. In the wake of every parent's worst nightmare, Kate and Chad rolled up their sleeves and chose to direct their efforts toward ending NF.

Unlike large charities with huge budgets and the ability to advertise on TV, PFF relies on community fundraising events such as their annual family jamboree. Last year at "Fam Jam," I had the experience of meeting a neighbor on my block. For more than fifteen years, our only interaction was a quick wave as our paths crossed. Coming together in an environment dedicated to improving the world, however, has nurtured a legit friendship!

Kate and Chad see each and every contribution that comes in. I asked Kate how it makes her feel to see hundreds of friends and neighbors coming together to support her family's efforts. She told me that the effect of this outpouring has been to "transform her pain into purpose." I feel blessed to be a small part of this amazing organization. Please visit www.pennysflight.org or reach out to me directly if you are interested in joining our efforts.

Earlier in the book, I encouraged you to surround yourself with positive people who share the belief that great things are possible. This is easily done by getting involved in one of the many wonderful organizations out there.

Another impediment to charitable giving is a feeling that the wants and needs out there are so great that any contribution I may make is of negligible value. I am reminded of the parable of the boy who encountered thousands of starfish washed up on the beach. He proceeded to throw them back into the water one by one before they perished. A man watching (instead of helping) him pointed out that the boy's efforts didn't matter because he couldn't possibly save all of them.

Nodding to the starfish in his hand, the boy said, "It matters to this one."

I know for a fact that the smallest charitable act can have untold positive ripple effects. Does it sound ridiculous when I say that a bag of Snickers changed the trajectory of my life? Perhaps—but it did. The feeling of pure surprise and happiness that it triggered was a first for me. It was a real boost. It established as fact that there are good forces out there that can lift me up. It was the starting point for positive beliefs.

By changing someone's external circumstances, we can change their beliefs. What we believe, in turn, changes our lives.

An example of belief-changing behavior was found in a study of elementary school children and teachers. Researchers randomly identified students in an incoming third grade class as belonging to three groups. The teacher (but not the students) was told that some of the students were "struggling" academically, some were of "average" intelligence, and a few of the students were "gifted."

At the end of the school year, the students labeled "gifted" had achieved the best grades in the class. This was clearly a function of the teacher's belief altering her manner and method of instruction for the "gifted" students.

Misguided Generosity

Not all sharing is good. Cousin Lloyd, who has never held a steady job, will be unlikely to make proper use of your gift to him.

Don't share what you cannot afford to lose. I learned this as a second-year law student. Randy, a classmate who was a new transfer student, was stressing out because his student loan check was delayed. It would take ten days to get sorted out. Unfortunately, he had already written checks to his new landlord for first and last month's rent plus security. Could I possibly lend him $5,000?

I did not have $5,000. I did, however, have access to my newly deposited student loan money, earmarked to pay my own tuition. You know there is a problem coming. At the time, I didn't. Professional students are great credit risks. Plus, I'd be seeing him every day. He couldn't avoid paying me—right?

Wrong! Turns out that "Randy" was not even a law student! He hung around the campus, cafeteria, and break areas for a few weeks cultivating targets. He walked away with a lot of money and was never caught!

I developed a rule which has served me ever since: I have never again made a gift or loan that I can't afford to lose. If a friend or family member asks for a loan, I apologize for not being able to and instead reduce the amount of the ask by at least one decimal point and offer this reduced amount as a gift.

Giving Love

Giving love to family, friends, and even strangers doesn't cost anything but is probably harder for most of us than sharing our stuff.

Both the Torah and the New Testament tell us to love thy neighbor as thyself. But I can barely tolerate my nasty neighbor or my annoying coworkers. I most certainly do not love the guy in the next cubicle who snaps his gum, chews with his mouth open, and hums to himself all day. Do I love my cousins, whose social media posts have revealed bewildering political positions? Do I even still love my spouse? He seems to become more annoying by the day. He certainly didn't act like this when we first met.

The answer to all "do I love" questions depends upon our definition of love. If it is an emotion or feeling, then the answer may change with the wind. If instead, it is a decision or an active verb, then the answer is within our control. To love someone is a volitional choice. To strive to love everyone is a practice.

In *The 7 Habits of Highly Effective People*, Stephen Covey tells the story of being on a train with a group of young children and their father. The children were running wild, and the father didn't seem to notice. This scene drove Mr. Covey bonkers.

After trying to ignore the children's disruptive and obnoxious behavior, he brought it to the father's attention. "Sir, do you see how your children are behaving? Can you please try to control them?"

Instead of taking offense, the father sadly agreed: "I am sorry—you are right. We just left the hospital where my wife just died, and I guess they don't know how to act or what to do. I don't either."

What do you think Mr. Covey's reaction was? He did a complete emotional 180-degree turn. In an instant, he went from seething anger to wanting nothing more than to be of some help to this group of strangers who just lost their wife and mother. Trying to sympathize or empathize with one another makes it easier to try to love them.

My life is more enjoyable because I make a conscious effort to love people. As an estate planning attorney, it is pretty easy to find things to love about my clients. I have the advantage of being able to ask broad, sweeping, and highly personal questions about their lives. My probing interviews about their childhoods and money habits result in good planning and also contribute to my ongoing empirical research into money behaviors.

Fostering meaningful and beautiful connections with people is, for me, as good as it gets. Pushing beyond the normal two-dimensional relationships we have with people in our daily lives has become a habit of mine. Sometimes with mixed results.

Some years back, a retired cop, Frank McKinley, came into my office to create a will. He was in his early seventies and a confirmed bachelor. In the course of going through his assets, I was moved to learn that his long-deceased mother was still listed as the beneficiary on his life insurance. He had no family and no clear idea who he wanted to leave his assets to. He had a friend who drove him to some of our meetings. He named this friend as both his health care proxy and power of attorney agent. The friend was also named executor of the will, which left the assets to a number of charities.

Over the years, Frank came to see me periodically, to tinker with the percentages going to the various charities. I came to believe that he really just wanted to come to my office for coffee (not his customary drink of choice) and a chat. There came a point when I hadn't heard from him in a while, so I called. He told me that he was very sick and didn't have more than a few months to live.

The thought of him being sick and alone in his apartment saddened me to no end. With no plan or forethought, I was moved to invite him to come live in my home until he felt better.

His response will stay with me forever: "You can go shit in your hat."

All right, then. That night, I told my husband how close he came to a live-in alcoholic patient with stomach cancer.

Frank came into my office one more time, and neither one of us mentioned my invitation to be housemates. We reviewed his will, and he gave me a sealed envelope with funeral and other instructions to be opened upon his death. No more than eight weeks later, I got the call that he died. The thought of him dying alone in his apartment brought me to tears.

It was the night of our tenth wedding anniversary and we splurged for dinner at the Jedediah Hawkins Inn on the North Fork of Long Island. I sobbed through most of the meal. Other diners must have thought Bill was breaking up with me. What an awful evening!

Back in the office Monday morning, I pulled Frank's file and opened his instruction envelope. It was filled with cash and a note that read, "Ann, please buy yourself something nice, from your crazy friend, Frank."

Wow—this gesture still bowls me over. I knew then that he didn't totally dismiss my overture to him. He was moved to let me know this with his final act on this earth. Even though he did not take me up on my offer to come live in my home, he let me know that it touched him. I hope that he felt less alone at the end, knowing that someone cared about him. I felt that Frank, in his own way, loved me back.

Our Anglo history of jurisprudence accords special weight to declarations made in the context of dying. This got me to thinking about what we can do now to better share what we have with those who will come after us.

One of the many pieces of advice from Stephen Covey that resonates with me is to "begin with the end in mind." He advised all of us to take a stab at writing our own eulogy. What do we want people to be able to say about our life once it's over? Modern self-help guides refer to this as a mortality consciousness. Morbid? Yes, but it is the ultimate in goal setting.

What do I want my life to have been about? Giving periodic thought to the end game immediately shifts our focus away from the unimportant nonsense that tends to fill our minds.

Some special people are able to dig down near the moment of death and offer words of guidance and comfort to those around them. I learned about one such individual from the business coach and motivational speaker Ed Mylett.

Mr. Mylett shared the story of his father's final hours of his battle with cancer. A longtime alcoholic, Ed Mylett Sr. had been sober for many years and served as a sobriety coach. As he lay in bed, struggling to breathe, his cellphone rang. He gestured for the phone. Upon recognizing the number, and over the protests of his family, he answered.

Through labored breathing, and a barely-there voice, he urged the caller to stay strong and stay sober. He died shortly after this call.

This story made such a huge impact on me. Here was someone who knew that he did not have long to live. With his very last bit of strength and conscious energy, he was moved to try to help his friend not give into a destructive temptation. This, for me, was a story of triumph. With what were literally his last breaths, he helped someone in need, while giving the rest of us a standard to aspire to. Well done!

I suppose that as an estate-planning attorney, for better or worse, I give more thought to my own mortality than most folks. I deal with crying, grieving family members on a weekly basis. I think about my own children, one day, dealing with my death. This will be the first rotten thing that happens to them where I won't be there to provide comfort and advice. I give a lot of thought to how I can make life's toughest hour easier for my loved ones.

Starting at the practical level is easiest. If you are a private person and are reticent to share the nature and extent of your finances with your loved ones, then at least make sure things are organized and accessible. Keep a binder or folder with current statements for all of your financial accounts. Social media passwords, online financial logins, and cryptocurrency-access instructions are all essential for your loved ones to have. Please don't let fear of your own mortality result in a huge, tangled mess for grieving loved ones.

This is far worse than moving out of a shared apartment and leaving your roommates with all of your junk and a big phone bill! I know that I don't want to go down in family history as a bad roommate. Give some thought to what your loved ones need to know and do in order to tie up your affairs. Does anyone owe you money? Do you wish for the debt to be forgiven? Do you have hidden cash or valuables?

I have had more than a few clients mistrustful of banks who insist on hiding cash in the house. Mr. Valentine was one such man. He advised me that there was $300,000 in cash in his home. I told him half-jokingly that I did not want to know exactly where in his home he kept it. I just wanted an assurance that it was in a locked safe or fireproof strong box.

No, it wasn't. He assured me though, that it was well protected. Fast forward five years. The Valentine children made an appointment to see me. Their father had not died, but he did suffer from dementia. He no longer knew their names—or his own. They had the house listed for sale and needed help attempting to protect the family finances in advance of their father's imminent admission to a nursing home.

They provided a list of assets that more or less matched up with the information in my file—with one exception. I asked about cash. The children were unaware of any cash beyond what was in their father's wallet. OMG.

After I shared my notes about the $300,000, the house was taken off the market and the children spent the next few months pulling up floorboards. No cash was ever found.

Mr. Valentine's mistrust of banks resulted in the very thing he feared. The money was forever lost.

If you happened to have purchased a Cape Cod–style home in Floral Park, New York, in 2018, you may be sitting on a windfall. Please promise me that you will put the three-step plan to work if you find the money. That is, after paying income taxes on it. Did you know that income taxes are owed on found money?

My beloved late grandmother, Lorraine, a.k.a. the slip-and-fall queen, unfortunately left a bit of a tangled mess upon her death. She was profoundly superstitious. She could not even utter the word cancer. She referred to it as "that bad thing."

My one and only attempt to discuss estate planning with her was met with a sharp rebuke that I was trying to hasten her demise. Respectful of her autonomy, I never raised the topic again. Our grief over her ultimate passing was punctuated with squabbles and hurt feelings. She left no will, no instructions, and an apartment full of hidden bank statements and stashes of valuables. I still shake my head at the gold necklace I found in a bag of fish food. Her profound fear of losing what she had was likely a result of growing up during the Great Depression. The sad thing is that her fear not only left a mess for the next generation, but it also prevented her from fully enjoying her life. Not only did she have plastic covers over all of her furniture, but she also had white sheets on top of all of the plastic—presumably to keep the plastic clean.

Those who can summon the courage to take steps to smooth the passing of life's baton should be remembered as a hero. At a minimum in this regard, we should all assemble an inventory of our stuff and a road map to gather it all. In the extra credit category is making our own funeral arrangements. Those of us who have planned funerals while in the throes of fresh grief know how painful it is. I can attest to some horrendous and very costly decisions while in this situation. This is not what I want for my children.

Every state in the US guarantees the payments made on pre-planned funerals. By making some practical decisions now, we are locking in costs, thereby saving a lot of money for our loved ones later. This is also a very kind and loving thing to do.

Making concrete plans for death is our final act as a parent. It is a natural and beautiful bookend to our happy and frenzied nesting behavior while expecting a baby. Parents can easily remember the planning and preparation of bassinettes, cribs, and nursery décor. We began our parenting journey with the fervent desire to surround our little ones with comfort, love, and safety. Don't we want to do what we can to smooth things over for them in what will be our final parenting act?

When we met our crying newborns, we did everything possible to comfort them. Thoughtful estate and life planning can go a long way to comforting our crying adult children as they begin their lives without us.

A thoughtfully crafted estate plan is truly a gift to our loved ones, which will protect them from evildoers, save them a many-months-long probate, and prevent their inheritance from arriving C.O.D. (ask someone over age 50) because estate taxes are owed. Yes, paying taxes is mandatory—but overpaying taxes is just plain stupid!

Secure in the knowledge that we have created a thoughtful, streamlined, and tax-efficient wealth delivery vehicle for the next generation, we are freed up to fully enjoy what will hopefully be many wonderful years ahead!

TAKEAWAYS

- A generous estate plan requires us to change the focus from *who* gets what to *how* they get it.
- All families are different. A one-size-fits-all estate plan usually fits no one.
- Get involved with a grassroots charity. You will experience the joy of seeing the effects of your contributions, while also providing a beautiful example to your loved ones.
- Your generous actions can't fail to cause wealth to come your way!

Afterword

Dear Readers,

Thank you for reading *The Smart Woman's Guide to Building and Protecting Wealth*. I hope that these pages have given you some ideas with which to achieve your wealth goals.

If you loved the book, it would mean a lot to me if you wrote an online review. This will help spread the word and educate others.

Estate and wealth planning should never be totally DIY, nor should it be totally outsourced. The documents that you can do on your own are available to you on my website: mylawyerann.com.

If you live in New York State, I would be delighted to work with you on your wealth protection and legacy planning. If you are out of state, I may be able to recommend someone for you to work with. I am in the process of developing a national referral network. To that end, if you wish to recommend someone who you think highly of, please let me know.

Please reach out if you are interested in having me as a speaker. I would also *love* to hear your money stories. Please know that your contact information will never be shared. My email is acarrozza@amcnylaw.com. Instagram: @mylawyerann.

I am sending you my profound thanks for reading as well as my sincere wishes for your future happiness and prosperity.

XO Ann

Index

U

V

W

Z